Folding the World

Sustaining a Changing World on a Finite Planet

Folding the World

Sustaining a Changing World on a Finite Planet

Anders Levermann
Potsdam Institute for Climate Impact Research, Germany

World Scientific

NEW JERSEY • LONDON • SINGAPORE • BEIJING • SHANGHAI • HONG KONG • TAIPEI • CHENNAI • TOKYO

Published by

World Scientific Publishing Europe Ltd.
57 Shelton Street, Covent Garden, London WC2H 9HE
Head office: 5 Toh Tuck Link, Singapore 596224
USA office: 27 Warren Street, Suite 401-402, Hackensack, NJ 07601

Library of Congress Cataloging-in-Publication Data
Names: Levermann, Anders author
Title: Folding the world : sustaining a changing world on a finite planet /
Anders Levermann, Potsdam Institute for Climate Impact Research, Germany.
Description: Singapore : World Scientific, 2026.
Identifiers: LCCN 2026004157 | ISBN 9781800618985 hardcover |
ISBN 9781800619180 paperback | ISBN 9781800618992 ebook |
ISBN 9781800619005 ebook other
Subjects: LCSH: Sustainable development | Human ecology--Economic aspects
Classification: LCC HC79.E5 L4724 2026
LC record available at https://lccn.loc.gov/2026004157

British Library Cataloguing-in-Publication Data
A catalogue record for this book is available from the British Library.

Die Faltung der Welt
Originally published in German by Ullstein Verlag in 2023.

For any available supplementary material, please visit
https://www.worldscientific.com/worldscibooks/10.1142/Q0558#t=suppl

Desk Editors: Kannan Krishnan/Gabriel Rawlinson

Typeset by Stallion Press
Email: enquiries@stallionpress.com

… I could be bounded in a nutshell and
count myself a king of infinite space …
Shakespeare, *Hamlet*

For
Christiane
Shiva and Ole
Max and Mascha

About the Author

Photo credit: Mathias Bothor

Anders Levermann (born 1973 in Bremerhaven, Germany) studied physics in Marburg, Berlin and Kiel. In 2002, he received his doctorate in theoretical physics from the Weizmann Institute of Sciences in Rehovot, Israel. He has been a researcher at the Potsdam Institute for Climate Impact Research for over 20 years, where he was heading the department for Sustainable Solutions and is now leading the department of Complexity Science. Since 2007, he has also been a professor of physics at the University of Potsdam, and between 2015 and 2023 he was a researcher at Columbia University, US. He has contributed to the reports of the Intergovernmental Panel on Climate Change (IPCC) for over 15 years and has authored more than 160 scientific articles, increasingly covering economic topics. His studies on the stability of the Antarctic Ice Sheet and the influence of rainfall distribution on economic growth were featured as cover stories in *Nature* in 2020 and 2022, respectively. Professor Levermann advises the German army on geoinformation systems, as well as an alliance of the international finance sector on zero-carbon strategies. He lives in Berlin, Germany.

Prologue

> Just saved the world. Can't leave anything to chance...
> I'll see you in the beginning, friend.
> *Robert Pattinson as Neil in "Tenet" (2020)*

Let's take a table-tennis ball. At first it is just a simple ball without feelings or desires, but if you stay with me, that will soon change. If this ball were in space, far away from the Earth and other heavy bodies such as the moon or even the sun, it would always fly straight ahead at the same speed[1]. If we take the mathematical-physical perspective of the table-tennis ball, we are only interested in where we are and where we are going next. We can build a coordinate system in which one of our axes always points forwards. This works because there is a direction that is always forwards. And because there are no forces acting on the ball, it never changes direction. It always flies straight ahead. Forward in its world.

We can make the ping-pong ball a little more interesting by giving it a value system that says: "Ahead is good, and further ahead is better." In this airless theoretical world, we would then have a happy ball, because it would improve at every moment. But even in this rather theoretical world of emotional ping-pong balls in space, simplified to the point of absurdity, happiness cannot last for all eternity. Because even in space, with its seemingly infinite extent, there is a limit – that of the universe. And before our lucky ball reaches it, it will most likely pass a planet, and then its free flight will change. Because then it will be deflected by the planet's gravitational pull.

---

1 For the pros: Before we launch the table-tennis ball into the void of space, we have of course made a small hole in it so that it doesn't explode when the air pressure from outside is relaxed.

If the ping-pong ball defines the direction that was previously forward as the only path to happiness, then something terrible will happen: It will become a sad ball. After it has crossed the aforementioned planet and has thus been diverted from its original path, it continues to fly undisturbed – but in a different direction. If it now defines its old forward as good, it will move further and further away from it and become increasingly unhappy. A good strategy for our ball would therefore be to change its value system and adapt to the new direction of flight.

Some might say that it shows a lack of backbone to change your value system – but still. The whole thing becomes even more complex when our ball is not the only one in the universe. What if the next distraction does not come from one of the distant planets, but other balls with their own value systems floating around in space, and our ball occasionally collides with one of them? Such a collision would dramatically change the direction of flight of both, until the next collision. Again, if our ping-pong ball only considers the one direction (the one it was pushed into life with) as good, then it is likely that collisions with other ping-pong balls will make it unhappy.

We need to take this absurd example a little further. Table-tennis balls in space fly in one direction until they hit something, and then they change direction according to the law of conservation of momentum, like balls on a pool table. But a ball that we throw up on Earth will not fly in the same direction; instead, it will constantly change direction. According to the force of gravity, it will perform a parabolic flight until it hits the Earth. At first, it will fly in the direction in which we threw it, but the Earth will immediately pull it under its spell and change its trajectory. With a fixed value system, it would again be doomed to sadness, and this shows above all that its movement on Earth is restricted and unfree. This is because our little fellows have feelings but cannot move on their own. So they are slaves to their environment, without any possibility of influencing their fate.

Let us now imagine the world as a world of active balls – of golden snitches like the one Harry Potter has to catch in order to win a

Quidditch match for his team. The golden snitch flies forward on its own and seems to have free will. In J. K. Rowling's book, for example, it flies in zigzags to escape its captor and thus follow its destiny. Let us now assume that our ping-pong balls can move freely and thus decide where they fly, but still have a fixed value system that was determined at the beginning, namely by the direction in which they originally flew. Now they will quickly escape the Earth and fly off in that direction. And since they can move themselves, they will always return to this direction. If they crash into a planet, they will try to get back on course afterwards and continue to head in the original direction. They will do the same if they collide with another ball. From the outside, this behaviour seems more like that of a fanatic, but the balls are getting happier and happier.

Unless there is an obstacle they can't get around, for example a crater in a planet, which they cannot get out of because they keep flying short-sightedly in the same direction without realizing that they will only crash into the same obstacle again. This kind of behaviour makes a snitch a stupid snitch. It becomes tragic when its short-term optimization of happiness takes it in the direction of the sun. Because then it will burn up.

What happens if we give the golden snitch not only the opportunity to move freely, but also the opportunity to decide which direction it likes? We can safely assume that it would not fly into a sun. But would it fly into space at all and continue straight on to the end of the universe? Maybe it would, but that would mean leaving all the other golden snitches behind. Some of the snitches would maybe choose this route. But if snitches needed air to survive, they would certainly not leave the atmosphere. They would respect the limits imposed by their nature and their environment and stay close to the Earth.

The snitch in Harry Potter even stays close to the playing field because the meaning of its existence is bound to the game. Other little golden balls may seek and find a different meaning. The question is, do we consider them unfree because they cannot leave the atmosphere? I believe they are no more unfree than a flock of birds that can move freely in the sky. It must not plunge into the ocean or fly into empty space, but there is infinite freedom between these natural boundaries.

In fact, it could even be that flocks of birds avoid each other and thus explore the sky and new food sources. I suspect that if two flocks of birds were released close together, they would each make their own

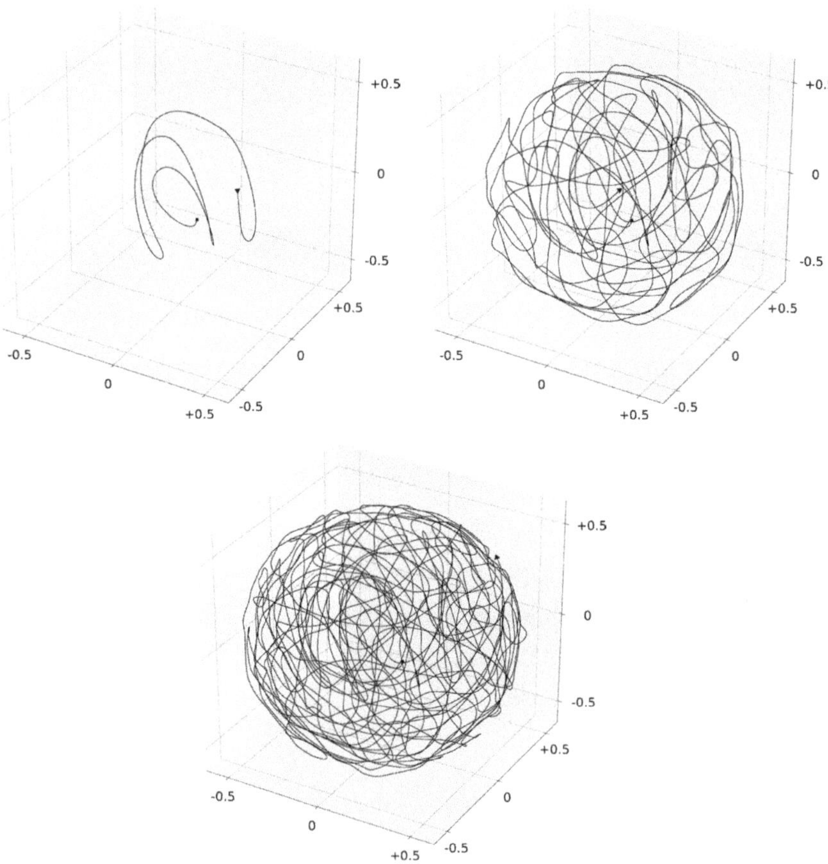

Figure 1. Illustration of the folding in a dynamic system. Shown is the path of a being that tries to find places where it has not yet been. It is therefore repelled by its own past and so strives forward. At the same time, it must remain in a finite space. It is aware of these natural limits and folds its path, its trajectory, whenever it comes close to the border back into the areas that are still free. Little by little, it explores the entire possible space. In doing so, it is faster than any systematic search in closing the remaining gaps in space.

path and fly apart as quickly as possible to avoid getting in each other's way. Because their habitat is limited and there are other flocks of birds, they are constantly forced to find new food sources and breeding grounds. Some may develop different methods of foraging and nest building in order to explore new habitats. In this way, diversity and creativity arise from the desire for freedom of individual flocks of birds and the limited space available. This is The Folding (Figure 1).

Contents

1 The Growth Dilemma

> This is not gonna end well.
> *Adam Driver as officer Ronnie Peterson in*
> *"The Dead Don't Die" (2019)*

The dilemma of motion and limitation has been in my mind for a very long time. It basically boils down to the question: Can there be infinite growth on a finite planet? Trained as a theoretical physicist, I have been researching physical climate problems for more than twenty years, and for over a decade now I have also been working on the economic aspects of the climate problem.

In the last four years, the world's leading scientific journal *Nature* has published two studies of my research group, both of them as cover stories – one on the physical stability of Antarctica and one on the economic costs of climate change. In this book, I combine considerations from both worlds – the natural sciences and economics. The finite nature of our planet and its resources is a fact. The dilemma arises when one is convinced – as I am – that continuous development is inevitable. Moreover, this further development must be free of restrictions in order to actually find effective solutions to new challenges.

I would like to offer here the narrative of folding, which I believe can replace the paradigm of unlimited and constant growth that prevails in large parts of our economy and our society as a whole. It is a new narrative, an alternative to the conviction that the solution to our sustainability problem can only be found through renunciation and a return to old ways of life.

Even though I believe that the new narrative offers orientation for a functioning society of the future, this book naturally cannot provide all of the solutions. I try to explain what the idea of folding can mean for some important areas of our society and show how the principle can be applied and how flexible it is.

I believe that the application of folding to the political and social shaping of our future can go a long way, and since we are already living much of this today, it will sound familiar to you to some extent. In a nutshell, folding always occurs where an actively developing system is confronted with limits. The suggestions I am making are precisely that – suggestions. Folding exists as a phenomenon even without these possible applications.

I don't use a single mathematical formula in the book,[1] but I do use mathematics. This need not put anyone off, because math is simply the language that some of us have learned to formulate thoughts. It has some advantages and some disadvantages. You can certainly express the thoughts written here in other ways than I have done, as I have already experienced with my wife and friends. I hope that the reader will do the same. They are mostly simple thoughts, what is new is their combination.

Although mathematical descriptions of reality are often associated with physical facts, mathematics is much more universal in the sense that it can be applied to all areas of life. It is a kind of "frozen logic." This means that if you transfer a fact into mathematics or represent it in mathematics, you can use its theorems and lemmas to arrive at new conclusions. Since mathematics is inherently consistent, the conclusions are always consistent with the assumptions. The only possible source of error lies in the transfer of reality into mathematics and back again. Mathematics represents truth. This makes it fascinating and naturally restricts it to situations in which there can be truth.

You will not need mathematics to understand this book and the concept of folding – I promise you that; rather, I believe that the mathematical concept of folding can be productive in rethinking

[1] Only in footnotes – a few.

the political and social shaping of the future, and I invite you to join me in this attempt. I wrote this book as a suggestion to provide a workable society for my children – to be able to live both on a healthy planet, but also in a free and democratic state of law – which is what I wish for them.

2 The Principle of Self-Amplification

Growth. Expansion. The point is, you're either appearing or disappearing.
Michael Douglas as Gordon Gekko in "Wall Street" (1987)

Before I explain the concept of folding in more detail and apply it to various areas of our life, I would like to introduce one important principle: self-amplification.

Self-amplifications are easy to understand, and we find them practically everywhere in our lives (Figure 2). What's more, they are at the centre of a dilemma that determines the political and social debates of our time like no other, and in some ways even sets the framework for them: the dilemma of infinite growth on a finite planet.

In fact, the entire world – physics, biology, psychology, society – can be viewed from the perspective of self-amplification processes, because they dominate the natural world around us as well as our societies and thus also our economic growth and our consumption of resources. It is therefore worth taking a closer look at the mechanism before thinking about how we can deal with it.

2.1 The Principle

The principle is wonderfully simple and universal[1]:

Self-amplification occurs when a quantity grows more strongly the larger it already is.

---

1 Simplicity and universality are the highest goals of scientific theory, alongside lack of contradiction, of course. This is summarized in the famous epistemological statement from scholasticism, which is sometimes referred to as Ockham's razor. William of Ockham described it in 1341 in his *Summa Logicae* manuscript.

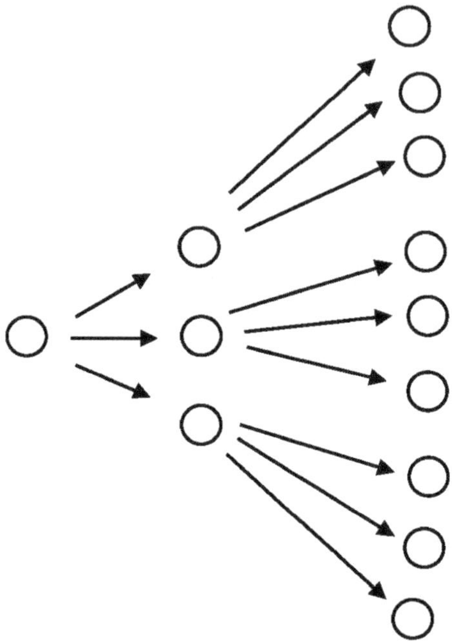

Figure 2. Simple illustration of self-amplification: In some atomic bombs a neutron splits a uranium atom, creating three more neutrons. This sets off a chain reaction or self-amplification, and the number of neutrons grows exponentially. We find similar mechanisms everywhere in nature, the economy and society – always when the increase in a quantity increases with the quantity already present: More rabbits mean more baby rabbits.

Or to put it plainly: More bunnies means more baby bunnies. The amount that grows can be material, like a bunch of cute rodents or dangerous viruses. But it can also be something virtual, like the money in my bank account or the value of Google. In digital media, we experience self-amplification when a rumour makes the rounds at breakneck speed or through YouTube videos, posts and songs that go viral. The fact that this process is referred to as "going viral" speaks for itself. The more people share something, the greater the likelihood that it will be shared further – whether by the users themselves on Bluesky by people ranting at the coffee machine in the office or by algorithms, as is the case with most other online platforms such as Instagram or TikTok.

The amount that grows can even be negative. In a stock market crash, companies' losses grow according to a self-amplification principle: The more the value of a share falls, the more people sell it, the supply on the market increases and the price falls further.

But slowly, let's illustrate some of the characteristics of these processes with a few simple examples to understand their importance and dynamics. In a viral disease, every virus that is not rendered harmless by the immune system is a source of more viruses. Without self-amplification, only viruses that we pick up from outside our bodies would make us ill, so their numbers in our bodies would only increase if we were around infected people. As soon as we moved away from them, the number of viruses in our bodies would stagnate. We would fall ill much less often and there would have been no COVID-19 pandemic. We would not be "infected." Instead, a viral illness would be like touching a hot plate: harmful to the extent that we have burned ourselves, but no more. In reality, once infected, the viruses develop a momentum of their own in our body. This has a number of consequences. For example, it is then almost irrelevant whether we ingest further viruses from outside, because their quantity inside of us is controlled by the dominance of self-amplification, not by further ingestion.

This is the first universal characteristic of self-amplification processes: Within a short time, they overwrite any other process that does not self-amplify. The absorption of viruses from outside is such an example. No matter how many additional viruses we take in from outside, as soon as the self-amplification process has started *in* our body, this uptake is overwritten by a much more rapidly increasing number of viruses. The course of the disease is determined by our immune system's fight against the viruses' own momentum.

Self-amplifications are very well understood mathematically and have a whole range of properties that they all have in common. Their development over time, for example, can be complicated in detail, but

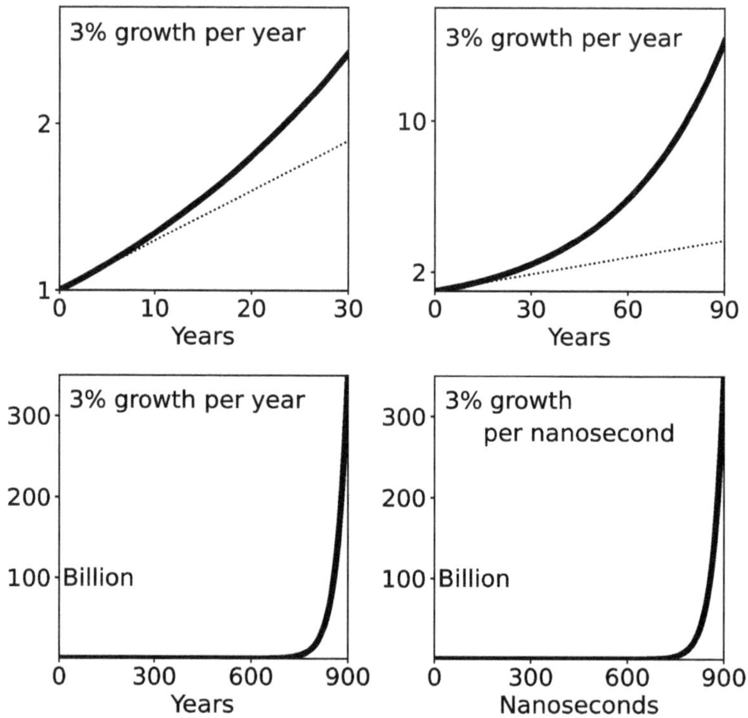

Figure 3. Self-reinforced and thus exponential growth of three per cent after different periods of time. If three per cent of the original value is added every year, the value has more than doubled after thirty years (top left), but the difference compared to linear growth (dotted line), where the same amount is always added, is still small. After three generations or ninety years, this difference can no longer be made up (top right). If the three per cent growth takes place on a shorter time scale, for example within a nanosecond, as in ultra-fast trading on the stock market (bottom right), then it is comparable to the annual growth after 900 years. This rate of increase is similar to the chain reaction in an atomic bomb.

in essence they always follow a so-called exponential function (Figure 3), which initially grows slowly, but then increases explosively from a certain point in time. Many people learned about these functions at school, but quickly forgot them, even though it is probably the most important mathematical function of their lives. Of course, you cannot see me smiling now, but I am aware that 99 percent of people get along very well without mathematical functions in their lives. Whether we know it or not, math is omnipresent and transcends everything. If aliens were to land on our planet, they would have the same math as we do, even if their bodies were made of gas or they were purely virtual intelligences. That is the beauty of this pure world of thought.

But back to self-amplification. At first you might think that it is the simplicity and universality of the process that makes self-amplifications so ubiquitous in our lives. The real reason, however, is their dynamic force. It leads to the fact that these processes always dominate the development of a system because they become stronger and stronger and thus displace other effects.

This is not self-evident, because not everything that occurs a lot in the world is the result of a self-amplification. The fact that our body consists largely of water, for example, is not due to a self-amplification process. Otherwise we would have to worry about accumulating more and more water in our bodies. This is not normally the case. Instead, we actually need to drink water constantly to keep our fluid balance stable.

This simple difference means that we have to deal with self-amplification processes in a fundamentally different way than with other situations in which there is simply a lot of something. Processes that self-amplify are powerful and dominant. And if we don't want them to dominate, then they need to be controlled. Not just in a pandemic.

The exponential growth of these self-amplification processes is reflected in the mathematical theory of dynamical systems by a positive so-called Lyapunov exponent. There is no need to understand this in detail, but the reciprocal of the Lyapunov exponent is a measure of time that roughly corresponds to the time in which the growing quantity doubles.[2]

If we stay with viral diseases, we can see that the principle also remains valid outside the human body. A disease spreads exponentially if a person infects more than one other person on average before going into quarantine. Even if we were talking about the same disease, this

---

2 For the pros: It is actually the time in which the quantity increases by the factor of the Euler number. The Euler number is 2.7182818 ... The doubling time is therefore always slightly shorter than the reciprocal of the Lyapunov exponent, to be precise, $1-\ln(2)$ smaller, i.e. around 30 percent.

is a completely different process than virus replication within the body. The number of people infected by one person, the so-called *R*-factor, has become sadly famous during the COVID-19 pandemic. It is the measure of the speed of spread. If you take this *R*-value minus one and multiply it by the reference period, for example one day or the period of time until a person either goes into quarantine or is no longer infectious, then you have the time in which the number of infected people doubles.[3] This means that if the *R*-value is greater than one, the number of infected people increases explosively because the Lyapunov exponent is positive.

This type of self-amplification process can be described as explosive growth, because the spread of viruses and bacteria in the body and the spread of diseases from person to person are mathematically practically identical to a physical explosion: In an atomic bomb, for example, the fission of each individual uranium atom nucleus leads to the release of three neutrons, which then fission further uranium atoms. If each of these neutrons causes a fission, the *R*-factor would be three, and if this happens within a period of, say, ten nanoseconds,[4] then the doubling time would be five nanoseconds.

Not only physical, chemical and biological phenomena are subject to this principle. Even processes that are controlled by our behaviour cannot escape it. As I said at the beginning: Every song that becomes famous, every video that goes through the roof is subject to this dynamic. They also dominate their environment and displace their competitors. This applies to the formation of monopolies by companies such as Google and Amazon as well as to the formation of opinion in society. In a certain sense, self-amplification can already be found in the famous statement "Nothing is as strong as an idea whose time has

---

3 The Lyapunov exponent is the *R*-value minus one: $\lambda = R - 1$.

4 The released neutron travels at a speed of about 10 million metres per second, or about 3 percent of the speed of light. A sphere with a critical mass of nuclear material has a radius of about 10 centimetres, or 0.1 metres. This results in a "travel time" of the neutron of 10^{-8} seconds.

come," which is attributed to Victor Hugo.[5] The key point here is "the time that has come," and Hugo is describing the coincidence of an idea with a certain historical context – in his case the idea of popular rule in the context of the impoverishment of broad sections of the population and the weakness of the elites. But the spread of the idea then takes the form of a self-amplification process, and this is how it develops its power in society.

The path to the climate crisis is also the result of at least two self-amplification processes: population growth and economic growth.

Although the development of the human population on Earth is highly complex, it is a self-amplification process. The mathematical principle transcends ethical, moral, religious, cultural and all other possible aspects: The net birth rate, i.e. the number of births minus deaths in a year, determines whether the number of people is increasing or decreasing. It is the Lyapunov exponent of population development. The complexity lies in which aspects of life determine this exponent – not in the self-amplification itself.

We humans have inhabited the Earth for around 300,000 years and have overcome one hurdle after another in the course of the climatically stable warm period in which we have found ourselves for more than 10,000 years in order to successfully assert our species against the competition. Slowly but steadily, we have not only climbed to the top of the food chain, but have also extended our lives further and further – thanks to medical advances, better food and hygienic living conditions. These are all improvements in every sense of the word, but they have led to exponential growth since the beginning of industrialization in the early 18th century, following a long period of little or no growth in the pre-industrial population.

---

5 It is often attributed to Victor Hugo, even though no proof has yet been found that the statement "Rien n'est plus fort qu'une idée dont l'heure est venue" was actually written by Hugo. But I think this only slightly diminishes its power. Especially since a very similar statement is made in his book *Histoire d'un crime*: "On résiste à l'invasion des armées, on ne résiste pas à l'invasion des idées." (One can withstand the invasion of armies, but not the invasion of ideas).

Of course, humans do not behave like viruses. Humans are rational beings who can make decisions and therefore influence the course of events. The question is therefore how this rapid growth can be influenced in a way that does not violate human rights, civil rights and civil liberties. It is clear that self-amplification processes cannot be controlled lightly. They must be confronted forcefully. More on this later.

Our economic growth is also a self-amplification process, because the basic mechanism of capitalism is self-amplification. At the microeconomic level of individuals and companies, this is very simple: The more capital a person or company has, the more they can invest or produce in order to gain capital – more capital leads to increased capital growth. Whether this is called interest or return is not really important.

At a national or even global level, this is somewhat more complex, but just as valid. In neoclassical macroeconomics, it is true that the growth of an economy saturates when the number of workers and technical progress stagnate. However, this thesis is based on the assumption that the growth rate decreases with capital and that an equilibrium is thus established.

Whether this is actually the case can and should be questioned. But let's start by assuming that it is true. If you look at the global economy, you can see that it is by no means in equilibrium. The economic strength of the US has grown at an average rate of around three percent per year since 1930, which corresponds to a Lyapunov exponent of one divided by 33 years and applied until the economic and financial crisis of 2008 and 2009 (Figure 3). The fact that economic production is not stagnating, contrary to the assumption, is justified in classical theory by the fact that population growth constantly increases the labour force and can therefore generate further growth. In this theory, economic growth would therefore either be linked to national population growth or would increase due to the relocation of labour to poorer countries. In addition, technological progress seems to increase indefinitely.

A successful explanation for the observed economic growth must therefore include explanations for the development of the labour force and technology. However, it is clear that more economic power leads to more economic growth and that we are therefore dealing with a self-amplification process.

2.2 Scales and Limits

If you give a physicist a problem, they will immediately and intuitively search for its scale – whether consciously or unconsciously: What does small mean and what is large, what is a lot and what means a few, what means fast and what means slow, in the respective context of the problem? The scales are often determined in some way by the limits of the system. Something that is large on a national scale does not necessarily have to be so on a global scale, but it probably is on a regional scale.

Our planet and our human nature set us limits and therefore scales. We could not survive permanently in an atmosphere with an air temperature of 40 degrees Celsius and 80 percent humidity.[6] We cannot process visual information that arrives faster than 18 frames per second. We rarely live longer than a hundred years. Limits restrict us, but they also give the world structure. Because an important consequence of these boundaries is that they create scale. Setting a limit clearly defines what is large and what is small. If we were to live indefinitely, one year of life would have less meaning and we would not be old at ninety. This also makes it clear that limits are not a bad thing *per se*. Limits generate scales and these in turn generate values.

Even an unlimited self-amplification process always has at least one scale, not in the quantity that grows, but in time. If you look at the illustrations of exponential functions (Figure 3), this means: Without a limit, a quantity can shoot up to infinity on the y-axis; on the x-axis, however, which represents time, there is a scale, namely the scale at

[6] Our body surface cannot cool down below the so-called "wet bulk temperature" through transpiration. Humans cannot survive in an environment where this is permanently above 35 degrees (Raymond *et al.*, 2020; Sherwood and Huber, 2010).

which the growth explodes, takes off in the y-direction and differs from a straight line. The reciprocal of the Lyapunov exponent determines the doubling time scale. The special thing about the self-amplification process is that it surpasses any quantitative scale that is set from the outside (y-axis). The time in which this happens is set by the time scale, and it determines the kink in the time development in which the initially linear growth becomes an ever steeper curve. For the atomic bomb, this scale is in the nanosecond range, for virus growth it is measured in days, for capital it is determined by the rate of return, and for population growth this time scale is determined by the length of successive generations and the number of births.

This again shows the danger of self-amplification. We need scales in order to imagine things and develop a feeling for a certain phenomenon or problem. It is difficult for us to judge dynamics that elude these scales.

In our everyday lives we are extremely good at intuitively grasping scales and estimating differences as long as they are part of our natural horizon of experience. A crooked picture immediately catches the eye because we can feel differences of millimetres. We know how far four kilometres are because we have already experienced that they are difficult to walk, but easy to travel by car or train.

This changes immediately when the scale is no longer part of our world of experience. Try to imagine four thousand metres upwards. That's more difficult. I have been researching the dynamics of the Antarctic ice sheet for over 15 years and I keep trying to intuitively imagine how far this ice sheet rises into the air. I can understand the four thousand metres, but I cannot feel them. I build bridges in my mind by thinking that it's about the height at which an airplane flies from Berlin to Munich, or half as high as an intercontinental airliner climbs into the air. But none of that really helps.

Now, for most people it is less important to imagine the Antarctic ice sheet. But the limits of our imagination become important when it comes to other questions. When we play the lottery, we weigh what for most people is an infinitely large prize of several million euros against the probability of 1:13,983,816.[7] Some people decide to play – others don't. The event "winning the lottery" happens from the perspective of a player who fills in exactly one box every week, on average about every 270,000 years. Even if you filled in a ticket, you would only have a reasonable chance of winning the jackpot if you had been playing for practically the entire Holocene. But the "there's a winner" event is close to 100 percent every week, and that probably makes many people invest the small amount, even if it's not a rational decision.

The lottery is a harmless everyday example of how we fail to assess scales that are not part of our realm of experience. But there are much more dramatic examples. Different people deal with the information that a dangerous accident at a nuclear power plant only occurs once every 10,000 years in different ways. The time scale is beyond our imagination because it is longer than anything we can experience in terms of time. The whole thing is further complicated by the fact that the scale of the disaster is also beyond our experience. Most of us have not yet experienced the effects of such terrible events directly and therefore find it difficult to assess the risk.

A frequently used way of defining risk is to multiply the size of a disaster by its probability. The greater the scale of the event, the greater the risk. Similarly, the risk increases with the probability of occurrence; the more likely the event, the greater the risk. In the case of the risk of a nuclear meltdown, we therefore have to combine a very small number, the probability, with a very large loss. Intuitively, this is virtually impossible. Some people reassure themselves by imagining the probability as practically zero. Zero is a number that is familiar to us and therefore tangible.

Others panic because the consequences of an accident would be unimaginably terrible. My guess is that many who actually feel fear, unconsciously increase their estimate of the probability, bringing it into a range they have experienced before. I think both intuitions are

---

7 The probability for the Jackpot in the Germany lottery, where 6 balls are picked out of a set of 49.

problematic because we can't imagine either the scale of harm or the scale of the small probability. It is important for our decision-making that we are aware of the limitations of our judgment.

In order to form an opinion that we can represent in social discussions and apply to our decisions, we need a feeling for the matter at hand. This is important not least because we have to derive decisions from the totality of our opinions. These are decisions about voting, but also about shopping and raising children. Sometimes imaginary bridges can help us to transfer things that we find difficult to imagine into our world of experience. If the probability of a nuclear reactor accident is once in 10,000 years and the 400 or so reactors currently in operation around the world can be considered independent of each other, then we should expect an average of one accident every 25 years worldwide.[8] This brings the problem into our world of experience and allows us to make an assessment. The three major accidents at Harrisburg in 1979, Chernobyl in 1986 and Fukushima in 2011, which have occurred since the first commercial nuclear power plant was connected to the grid in 1956, roughly match this figure.[9]

Becoming aware of the limitations of our imagination is not only important because we make (political) voting decisions. Above all, it plays a decisive role in our daily discussions about societal issues.

Unlike nuclear power plants, where the damage is so extreme that it cannot be allowed to happen, it can be problematic to make decisions on the basis of a discussion in which only the extreme edges of an issue are considered. This is a popular way of avoiding decisions that may be right and fine as long as a "reasonable level" is maintained. To name just one example: Arguments are often made against vegans by pointing to vegan mothers whose children are deficient in nutrients because of

---

8 If the probability of an accident per year is $p = 10^{-4}$, then the probability of an accident occurring with $N = 400$ reactors is: $P_N = 1 - (1 - p)^N$. This can either be calculated directly or with a Taylor series for small p as $P_N \approx N \cdot p = 1/25$ years.

9 Of course, this is only a rough estimate: In these 66 years, 400 power plants were not always connected to the grid. Safety is distributed differently and so on and so forth. The point here is to illustrate the mental bridge that can be used to bring the incomprehensible 10,000 years into a tangible and realistic order of magnitude without completely misdescribing the problem.

the strict diet. However, the fact that such – extremely rare – cases occur is not at all an argument against a sensible vegan lifestyle. Just how inane this type of argument is can be seen from the fact that we do not take a similar stance against the consumption of alcohol in the public debate. Since alcohol – unlike a vegan diet – has a long cultural tradition, we accept the downsides – even though the harmful and even fatal consequences of alcohol consumption in our society are a serious problem that can also be quantified in terms of costs – and the number of people harmed and killed by alcohol far outweighs the cases in which vegans cause serious damage to their health.

The issue of pushing arguments in a discussion to the extremes is not trivial, as this strategy is usually used to create propaganda against something that we as a society could possibly easily agree on if we did not fall for this manoeuvre. Another – of many – examples is the discussion about speed limits in Germany. For years, surveys have shown that the majority of the population is in favour of this (as are almost all countries in the world). Nevertheless, opponents argue with the completely exaggerated claim that this threatens their freedom, one of the political foundations of our society. One can understand how "extreme" this argument is if you consider which events really did put an end to freedom – the Nazi era, the building of the Berlin Wall – and that our liberal way of life has not really been damaged even by the drastic restrictions imposed during the coronavirus pandemic. Whatever you think of the speed limit, the freedom argument seems questionable, even when looking at other countries. Neither the French nor the English would describe themselves as "unfree," and the Americans, with their sometimes almost obsessive love of freedom, even have a particularly strict speed limit. I could cite many more examples to show that it can help to recognize propaganda by keeping the underlying scale in mind.

Scales are important and helpful in understanding if and when a self-amplification process can become dangerous. It doesn't feel particularly powerful at first when you get one percent interest on your savings account. The reason is that with a Lyapunov exponent of one percent per year, the doubling time scale is one hundred years. Compared to the five nanoseconds of the atomic bomb, this is much, much slower. Added to this is the devaluation of money through inflation. This means that in our lifetime we will hardly feel the self-amplification on our bank account.

But if you are a broker trading on the stock market with an algorithm in the nanosecond range, then self-amplification is actually tantamount to an explosion of an atomic bomb. It leads to profits that arise from previous profits, and this has consequences, because this self-amplification on the stock market really "explodes," so to speak, the inequality between an employee, who receives the same salary every month and can therefore only achieve linear growth, and the broker, whose wealth is moving further and further away from the majority of society.

Comparable processes manifest themselves on the real estate market with similar consequences. The time scale, i.e. the reciprocal of the Lyapunov exponent, lies between that of the savings account and that of nanosecond trading at the stock exchange. And here the social purpose of trading is initially even more obvious. Buying and renovating a property costs a lot of money. As soon as these investments are offset by rental income, they result in a profit. This in turn can be reinvested, for example in another property or in other profitable businesses. There seems to be nothing wrong with this incentive principle at first; it benefits the people who own the properties, but could also benefit those who can live in them. However, we are also seeing in the real estate market that the self-amplification momentum has no limit and is getting out of hand (more on the problem of the real estate market in Section 8.2).

All three examples, interest on bank accounts, rental income in the real estate sector and nanosecond gains on the stock market, are part of the self-amplification processes that are part of our economic growth (I will talk about others later). They differ in one important component, namely the time scale of growth, and this is crucial. Because depending on how the growth turns out on the time scale, it has consequences for our society that can be serious. That's why we need to talk about scales.

One consequence of the exponential growth that our economy and population have been experiencing for several centuries is that this growth is linked to the burning of fossil fuels. For many, the big question is therefore whether it will be enough to decouple economic growth from the destruction of our environment – for example by relying on new energy sources – or whether we have to stop economic growth itself completely. Scales are important for my proposal to resolve this dilemma through the new paradigm of folding.

2.3 Demarcation and Cluster Formation

So far, this chapter has dealt exclusively with a special class of self-amplifications, explosive growth. However, there are at least two other types that are extremely important. One is self-amplifying clustering. I will discuss the third, the tipping point, in Chapter 3.

Self-amplifying clustering occurs
when an accumulation gains an even
greater attraction as it becomes larger.

This process is also mathematically universal and has existed since the beginning of time. It too can refer to something material, such as stardust, or to something virtual, such as political opinion.

One example: In the early stages of our universe, randomly formed small clusters of "cosmic dust" had enhanced gravity compared to its direct vicinity and thus attracted surrounding matter. These slowly condensed into stars and planets. They thus became heavier and heavier, had more and more gravity and slowly but surely sucked up all the matter in their surroundings, so that our universe now consists largely of clumps of matter in an otherwise empty space. We live on one of these clumps of matter and decide how we want to shape our lives.

The fact that we can do this is again the result of self-amplification, because evolution is also a clustering process. The species that is best adapted to its environment survives. It can reproduce the most because its adaptive advantage gives it better food options or a lower mortality rate, for example. Even without a physical battle with its competitors, it can prevail in the long term. This means that living nature, as we perceive it around us, has grown out of self-amplification processes. Self-amplification acts here like a sorting process. Whoever grows the fastest wins, depriving their competitors of food and habitat. This process actually reduces diversity by weeding out less well-adapted species.

As in the case of the explosion, size also increases exponentially in the case of clustering, but this is more difficult to identify, and the increase is usually limited. In the case of star formation, it is the size of the stars that initially increases exponentially, but is then limited by the availability of cosmic dust. Natural selection of species is limited by habitat, but it also initially follows an exponential function.[10]

We also encounter processes of clustering in our everyday lives, for example in urbanization. More and more people are deciding to move to cities. There are many reasons for this. However, some of these reasons are related to the fact that many people already live in the city. More people mean more cultural and economic opportunities and therefore more and more diverse job opportunities. Whatever the reasons: If, during any phase of urban development, the increase in the number of people rises with the number of inhabitants, then it is a self-amplification process. Accordingly, urban development is often studied using so-called gravity models. Although people are not portrayed as mindless particles of matter, it is assumed that their decision to live in a particular city becomes more likely as the city's

[10] Due to the limitation, the corresponding differential equation (with a so-called logistic equation on the right-hand side) is $\frac{dx}{dt} = \frac{x}{\tau} \cdot (A - x)$. Here, x is the variable that grows during clustering, $1/\tau$ is the Lyapunov exponent and A is the limit beyond which x cannot grow. Initially, i.e. for small $x \ll A$, this behaves in the same way as the differential equation of exponential growth $\frac{dx}{dt} = \frac{x}{\tau}$, but it behaves differently the moment the limit becomes relevant, i.e. x grows into the vicinity of A.

size increases. This assumption is not uncontroversial, but it is one way of understanding the phenomenon.

The key point is that self-amplification in this case does not necessarily lead to an explosion, because the number of people who can move to the city in the first place is limited. It can be limited by the size of the population in the surrounding area or, if they can also come from further away, by the number of people who are allowed to live permanently in the country. The fact that the quantity is limited means that something different happens than with the explosion. An agglomeration occurs. In this case, self-amplification dominates the dynamics of the system even more, because it directly weakens the competitors. When a city grows, it not only becomes larger, it also deprives the surrounding places of the opportunity to grow larger. The Lyapunov exponent can be interpreted here as a kind of attraction that a city exerts on its surroundings. Urbanization has long been a strong trend in many parts of the world, and some estimates predict that more than 80 percent of the world's population will live in cities by 2050. This trend also has enormous consequences for the way we have to assess climate phenomena. It is fundamentally different if a natural disaster occurs in an area where people live more or less evenly distributed, compared to a city where people are concentrated and dependent on the supply from large-scale agriculture and production and the necessary supply routes. The type of disruption is fundamentally different in both situations.

Urbanization aside, I think that clustering currently plays the biggest role in society through opinion formation. Thanks to the free choice of information media that the internet provides, but also thanks to the algorithms behind search engines that control digital content, we are increasingly obtaining information only from media that reflect our opinion or are at least consistent with our opinion. Filter bubbles are emerging – almost closed spaces in which we increasingly select information in such a way that it supports our beliefs. We are increasingly reinforced in our own opinions and confronted less and less with other viewpoints.

Until the introduction of private television in Germany in the 1990s, an overwhelming majority of the population watched either the *Tagesschau* on ARD or *Heute* on ZDF.[11] This had two advantages over news production in the media landscape today: Firstly, there was a kind of universal information canon; it could be assumed that anyone who followed political and social events closely would access more or less the same minimal set of news and information. The canon was created by the selection of editorial teams in the publishing houses and television stations. Though, the obvious disadvantage was that people were dependent on these editorial teams. The second advantage was that all information generally met certain quality criteria or at least the quality was attributable to a news team. News had to be well-researched, clearly presented and as politically neutral as possible. In Germany, political neutrality in public broadcasters is also ensured by supervisory bodies in which the most important social groups are represented. It goes without saying that this news was not and could not be completely objective, and the language used in these news programs was dry and downright boring.

This changed in Germany in 1984, when the television landscape became more diverse with the emergence of private broadcasters. Suddenly it was all about market share and ratings, which had an impact on the quality of the content. Unlike in the USA, where Fox News, a television station, was founded explicitly with the aim of helping a particular party to power, the politicization of private broadcasters in Germany has hardly played a role to date. In any case, people started to choose their information source and society started to diverge with respect to their informational basis.

The most fundamental change, however, occurred when the internet gradually became the main source of news at the beginning of the 21st century. The algorithms of search engines, but above all social networks, which have become the first and sometimes only source of news for large sections of the population, ensure that more and more people access information and news that corresponds to their filter bubble,

[11] German daily evening news in government-sponsored TV stations comparable to the BBC in the UK.

i.e. that represents an increasingly narrow spectrum of topics and opinions. As a result, they enter into a self-amplification cycle that is based on cluster formation. In addition, especially in social networks, news often comes from dubious sources or is openly false: fake news. (And, of course, the very strategy that I described above as propaganda is often used, i.e. stirring up public opinion against something by scandalizing marginal phenomena.) This means that most of us are not only becoming more and more one-sided in our information, depending on the political camp, but parts of society are also losing touch with reality and becoming susceptible to conspiracy myths. We can directly observe how dangerous this can be for societal cohesion by considering the example of the US over the past several decades.

On the one hand, the self-amplification process in informational filter bubbles means that we become increasingly certain of our opinions – an effect that can turn into radicalization in extreme cases. On the other hand, it leads us to ban other opinions from our information bubble. In closed spaces, a fixed set of opinions are formed. Clustering becomes a demarcation and determines our purchasing and voting behaviour. We seem to live on different planets.

2.4 Limits We Cannot Ignore

We find it difficult for us to imagine certain limits, and that can be dangerous. But ever since the Club of Rome, led by Dennis Meadows, published its famous *Limits to Growth* report in 1972, we have known that our way of life will bring us towards the limits of our planet. Although they have been discussed and, in some cases, quantified by scientists from all disciplines in the fifty years that have passed since then, these limits have been largely ignored in politics and society. Most political decisions, in which at least an attempt to avert impending catastrophes is recognizable, come late and seem half-hearted.

Let us first take a brief, more recent look at these boundaries. In an article published in the journal *Nature in* 2009, my colleague Johan Rockström and an international team of scientists proposed identifying and quantifying certain so-called "planetary boundaries" (Rockström *et al.*, 2009). If we do not do this, they argue, we will cause environmental damage and consequences that we "cannot accept." Which immediately leads to the next question: What does "cannot accept" mean?

According to the authors, we "cannot accept" it if existing environmental conditions on Earth change to such an extent that they endanger human life in its current form or even make it impossible. Since 2009, Rockström together with a number of world-renowned scientists have updated the assessment of the state of our advancement towards and across these planetary boundaries three times. Together with the reports of the Intergovernmental Panel on Climate Change, the World Meteorological Organization and countless others, this work has convinced increasingly large parts of countries like the UK and Germany that crossing these boundaries really is not acceptable.

The conditions that are vital for us include not just a relatively stable climate with its complex subsystems (monsoon systems, North Atlantic Current, etc.) but also the global availability of drinking water, the presence of certain substances, the complex interplay of a variety of species and much more. For most of the past 10,000 years these conditions were present. This was the Holocene, the geological epoch with its long-lasting stability that allowed our civilization to develop into our present way of life: from the biface to the smartphone.

Based on our understanding of the Earth's climate dynamics and the planetary constellation in our solar system (more on this below), we know that the Holocene would have continued for several tens of millennia. *Would have continued.* Because since industrialization humans have become a geological force. In the past two centuries, we have changed our environment to an extent that requires a new branding. We have forced the Holocene which should have lasted another 50,000 years into a new era: the Anthropocene. We are living in a time of man-made geological change.[12]

---

[12] Nobel laureate Paul Crutzen, who proposed the term Anthropocene, was also involved in the initial article published by Rockström.

Rockström and his colleagues have identified nine physical, chemical and biological processes that are relevant to the changing environmental conditions of the Anthropocene:

- Climate change
- Species loss (land and sea)
- Intervention in the nitrogen and phosphorus balance
- Ozone layer depletion
- Acidification of the oceans
- Global fresh water consumption
- Land use
- Chemical pollution
- Atmospheric pollution with aerosols

Some of these anthropogenic changes are already so far advanced that the systems they affect are irreversibly changing or have already changed: Climate change, the rapid decline in biodiversity and the change in the nitrogen cycle are already having a lasting impact on the resilience of natural systems.

Some of these processes exhibit a threshold behaviour (so-called tipping processes). If a threshold is reached, the system destabilizes. In physics, destabilization is a process that progresses independent of further external perturbation. That means that if a warming threshold has been passed the system will collapse even if the warming does not continue. Examples include the ice sheets in Greenland and West Antarctica, the oceanic heat pump in the Atlantic and the Amazon rainforest. Other processes become gradually more dangerous the more they increase – this applies, for example, to dwindling biodiversity. In many cases it is not possible to determine the exact position of the threshold at which the increasing change would have concrete, unstoppable consequences.

In all cases, the authors of the *Nature* article suggest that the global community should agree on specific values that we should no longer exceed in order to ensure that the environmental conditions on Earth necessary for us humans and our way of life are maintained in the future. They call these the "planetary boundaries." The planetary boundaries represent a safety margin that should be maintained relative to the thresholds or ongoing changes in order to prevent catastrophic consequences. To use an image: The thresholds at which systems break down forever are the abyss; if we take a step here, we fall. The planetary boundaries would be a kind of fence that is placed a few metres away from the abyss, for example, to prevent us from reaching the abyss in the first place.

In order to determine such planetary boundaries, i.e. a safe distance within which we do not reach dangerous thresholds, we need certain social rules for dealing with risk and uncertainty.[13]

For example, we now know that at a CO_2 concentration of 450 ppm, a number of systems, such as Greenland and the West Antarctic, are very likely to tip over irrevocably. The planetary boundary that Rockström and colleagues propose for the CO_2 concentration is therefore 350 ppm.

Of course, it is debatable whether the limit has been set too cautiously, as we are now at about 425 ppm, and even if the consequences of climate change are visible everywhere, our systems are still holding up. Independent of whether one agrees with the 350 ppm planetary boundary, the magnitude of the risks that are at play makes it reasonable to follow the so-called *cautionary principle* and keep a sufficient distance from the dangerous limits. With all the values we agree on as limits, the questions always arise: What can be endured by humanity? By vegetation? By other species? Where exactly are the limits in each case?

While it is difficult to make predictions with certainty about the various physical systems and to set correspondingly safe limits, one thing must not be forgotten: That our way of life brings us up against limits where our environment changes with painful, perhaps even catastrophic consequences is a hard, absolutely immovable fact. This fact is the hard wall against which the ping-pong ball from the prologue inevitably crashes. We will reach such limits at some point. And unlike

[13] This is roughly how Rockström *et al.* (2009, p. 473) put it in *Nature.*

the ping-pong ball, we will be severely deformed, and in the worst case even destroyed, by such an impact. For example, at some point certain resources will no longer exist: It is absolutely irrevocable that we will have to stop extracting raw materials completely at some point in time. We will eventually only be able to use what grows back or what we have recycled. And at some point, the atmosphere will be so full of emitted CO_2 and the Earth will warm up so much that we will feel the consequences as unbearable (more on this in Chapter 3).

We are dealing with two types of limits. Firstly, the amount of material we consume is decreasing. Secondly, the Earth and its atmosphere represent a limited space that we are continuing to fill with carbon dioxide. We are currently polluting the atmosphere, the ocean and the land to an ever more threatening extent, as if the environment were a landfill. These landfills, like a real landfill, will eventually be full.

With this in mind, the US economist and Nobel Prize winner Elinor Ostrom proposed a model back in 1990 for how these *commons*, which are only available in limited quantities, can be used fairly and sustainably at a local level. Later, Ottmar Edenhofer from the Potsdam Institute for Climate Impact Research suggested transferring this idea to a global level. Careful handling of the limited *global commons* requires management, a strategy to be negotiated globally, at the level of the global community – very much in the spirit of a "world domestic policy" proposed by the German chancellor Willy Brandt many decades earlier. In the following chapter, I will first take a closer look at the boundary that is important for climate change.

3 The Folding Limit of the Climate

> It's like riding a psychotic horse towards
> a burning stable.
> *Robin Williams as Armand Goldman in*
> *"The Birdcage" (1996)*

Let us have a look at climate on Earth – why it is changing and what we have to do in order to avoid more dangerous changes.

3.1 Ice Ages and Warm Stages

For more than a million years, the Earth has gone through a natural cycle of alternating ice ages and warm periods with great regularity. The word *natural* is used here because this climate oscillation is driven by solar radiation and not by humans. The alternation of ice and warm periods does not occur, as one might think, because more or less solar energy reaches the Earth; it therefore has nothing to do with how close the Earth is to the sun. The decisive factor is the seasonality of the radiation. Due to the inclination of the Earth's axis of rotation, the amount of solar radiation changes across seasons. Since this inclination changes over the course of tens of thousands of years, the seasons also change. If the warming of the northern hemisphere in summer is not sufficient to melt the snow that has fallen in winter, then the reflective power of the white snow is so strong that the Earth cools down. The winter snow falls on top of the snow left over from the previous year, and slowly but steadily an ice sheet forms in North America and Eurasia – an ice age begins.

The ice age cycle is therefore determined by the fluctuating tilt of the Earth's axis in relation to the sun, and this oscillates with a period of around 100,000 years. Normally, the warm periods in this cycle are only about 10,000 years long.

It was around this time, 10,000 years ago, that the Holocene, the most recent warm period on Earth, began. It is "our" warm period. Since this geological epoch, the climate has been very stable, which has enabled us humans to live on Earth and develop our culture and civilization. Now, with its 10,000-year Holocene, the Earth would actually be ready for another ice age.

3.2 Radiative Balance and the Greenhouse Effect

Fortunately, this time we are in an abnormally long warm cycle, so the next ice age would not occur for another 50,000 years. I use the subjunctive here because we humans have been interfering with the natural cycle for some time and have most likely already prevented the next ice age.

The description of the glacial cycles is just one example of our understanding of past climate events. The basic physical understanding of the Earth's radiative balance is the reason that the statement that humans are warming the planet is irrefutable. It is not climate research, but physics that provides this foundation. The corresponding processes are very deeply understood, and accordingly there is no longer any uncertainty about the relationships. The fact that an accumulation of carbon dioxide and methane in the atmosphere increases the temperature of the planet is based on the laws of quantum physics and thermodynamics (or statistical physics), which have been known for more than a hundred years and are tested anew every day. You confirm quantum theory yourself every day when you use your cell phone or switch on your computer, and thermodynamics when you wipe the water vapour off the mirror after showering. All these pillars of modern physics are firmly in place, and they teach us the fundamentals of climate change.

The radiative balance is the difference between the energy that radiates onto Earth from the sun minus that which radiates from the Earth back into space. The back radiation is given by the famous Stefan–Boltzmann law and increases with a rising temperature on Earth. Thus Earth is warming under the solar insolation until it is warm enough to radiate enough energy back into space to be in equilibrium. Greenhouse gases shift this radiative balance by sending back energy that is on its way out into space back to Earth's surface. So Earth has to increase its temperature to find a new balance. When the Earth is in quasi-equilibrium, as it was during the past 10,000 years, before the Industrial Revolution, this balance is basically zero.

From quantum physics we know the absorption and emission spectra of the molecules CO_2 (carbon dioxide) and CH_4 (methane) and also those of water vapour, H_2O. We know that these molecules are invisible, and in physical terms this means that they do not absorb visible light. They let it through. Due to its extremely high temperature, the sun mainly emits visible and ultraviolet light. This is why sunlight is not absorbed by the atmosphere, but reaches Earth's surface and heats it up. The Earth, by contrast, is much colder than the sun and therefore radiates mainly in the long-wave infrared spectrum.[1] In the infrared spectrum, however, CO_2, methane and water vapour molecules are no longer permeable. Instead of letting this so-called thermal radiation[2] through into space, they absorb it and emit it again in all directions. As a result, some[3] of the energy returns to Earth and further heats it up.

1 Of course, the Earth also emits radiation in the visible spectrum, as we can see it in space. But a large part of the spectrum is in the infrared. Essentially, the radiation spectrum of a body is determined by its temperature and follows Planck's radiation law, whereby the total energy emitted per second follows the Stefan–Boltzmann law. This law plays a fundamental role in the discussion about the possibility of a (limited) runaway greenhouse effect. The reason for its importance is that it represents a very strong stabilizing feedback, not least because the radiated energy power increases with the fourth power of the absolute temperature of the radiating body.

2 If you have an infrared lamp at home, you can probably understand why this part of the electromagnetic spectrum is called thermal radiation.

3 Basically half of it.

Water vapour and other greenhouse gases warm the Earth's temperature – without this natural greenhouse effect, the global average temperature would be only –18 degrees Celsius; the Earth would not be habitable for us humans. The greenhouse effect is therefore initially a natural phenomenon; it not only plays a role in understanding the most recent anthropogenic[4] warming, but is just as central to understanding the temperature of Venus as our ice age cycles on Earth.[5]

Since the beginning of industrialization, when we started burning fossil fuels and released huge amounts of additional carbon dioxide into the atmosphere, we have been turning the dial on the natural greenhouse gas effect; we are "polluting" the air and thus increasing its greenhouse effect, causing the Earth's climate to warm up unnaturally.

So far, I have only described the first direct radiative component of the greenhouse effect. More greenhouse gases in the atmosphere increase the temperature of the planet. For every doubling of the carbon dioxide concentration in the atmosphere, the temperature increases by just over one degree Celsius.[6]

In response to this warming, the atmosphere reacts with the first so-called feedback: A warmer atmosphere can hold more water vapour than a colder one. This law is also not an invention of climate researchers, but was discovered even before the incredibly successful theory of thermodynamics was formulated. The Clausius–Clapeyron law of 1834 describes the vapour pressure curve as a function of temperature and is proven time and again by anyone who wears glasses and comes inside from the cold outside in winter: The glasses fog up because the cold atmosphere created by the cold glasses can no longer

[4] i.e. caused by humans.

[5] The shift in the seasonality of solar radiation described above is the cause of the formation of an ice age. The direct consequence of this is the formation of ice sheets. The planet cools down due to the increased reflection of solar radiation by the ice. However, the Earth then experiences an additional cooling of almost the same magnitude due to a change in the greenhouse effect: A colder ocean absorbs more carbon dioxide from the atmosphere, which is no longer available to warm the Earth, and it cools down further. The ice age is complete.

[6] 1.1 degrees Celsius.

hold the water vapour that the warm air inside the room can carry. The water vapour condenses into water droplets on the glasses – rendering us blind for a few moments.

The reverse happens when greenhouse gases warm our atmosphere. The water vapour content of the atmosphere increases – simple cooking-pot physics or thermodynamics. Since water vapour, as described above, is also a greenhouse gas, the additional water vapour in the atmosphere increases the temperature of our planet by an additional one and a half to two degrees for every doubling of the carbon dioxide content via the greenhouse effect. With these two effects alone, we therefore arrive at 2.5 to 3 degrees of global warming for every doubling of carbon dioxide in the atmosphere.

Like all physical systems on Earth, the climate is complex and there are other effects that are triggered by these processes. However, they are much weaker. Another feedback effect, for example, is the so-called ice-albedo effect: The melting of snow and ice masses on Earth leads to less solar radiation being reflected into space. The dark ocean under the ice around the North Pole or the dark land under the snow cover of Canada and Siberia absorbs the sunlight and warms itself and therefore the planet even more. Clouds also play a role because they change dynamically, and the dynamics of cloud formation are highly complex. They represent the greatest uncertainty in the calculation. Despite this uncertainty, the effect of clouds is relatively small compared to the powerful and fundamental contributions of the direct greenhouse effect and the first thermodynamic feedback from water vapour.

These feedbacks result in the so-called climate sensitivity: the extent to which the climate warms when the concentration of CO_2 in the Earth's atmosphere doubles. It has been and continues to be investigated using various methods over many decades. But because the main part is explained by the direct greenhouse effect and the first thermodynamic feedback, the result is always practically the same: The Earth warms by around three degrees for every doubling of carbon dioxide. That is Earth's climate sensitivity.

3.3 Tipping Points and Abrupt Transitions

The greenhouse effect is not a self-amplifying process, but a consequence of self-amplifications in economic and population growth and the associated emission of carbon dioxide. However, risks that imply self-amplifications also contribute to climate change. These are abrupt transitions, so-called tipping processes. They are self-amplifications that take a course different to the explosions and clustering described in Chapter 2; like these, however, tipping processes can also be found in physical, biological, chemical, psychological or social situations. Tipping points can be defined as follows[7]:

A system reaches a tipping point when its evolution is dominated by a self-amplification until it reaches a qualitatively different state.

The term "qualitatively different state" is not really clearly defined. It serves to distinguish the change from a mere quantitative difference. In most cases the difference is quite straightforward.

The Greenland Ice Sheet

Greenland, for example, currently carries an ice sheet that is on average three kilometres high. If the Greenland ice sheet were to lose ten percent of its ice volume, this would cause global sea level to rise by 70 centimetres. That would be a major change and a problem for many coastal cities. But it would be a quantitative rather than a qualitative change for the ice sheet, because there would still be an ice sheet and it would obey the same physical laws as it does today. An ice-free Greenland is something fundamentally different. When the ice sheet

[7] This dynamic definition was proposed in 2012 (Levermann *et al.*, 2012) and is now used worldwide (McKay *et al.*, 2022). The original definition of tipping elements was formulated from the perspective of societal consequences (Lenton *et al.*, 2008). It is very important and widely used. I am not using it here because it is quite complicated and is not intended from a dynamic perspective. However, it essentially results in the same list of possible tipping elements.

has completely melted, Greenland will have a new quality, because then it will simply be a large island and no longer one of two major ice masses on Earth. The same applies to Antarctica.

For a tipping process to take place, two conditions must always be met: There must be self-amplification, and this must dominate the dynamics, i.e. it must be stronger than possible stabilizing feedbacks.

The self-amplification process that generates the tipping dynamics of the Greenland ice sheet is a feedback between the height of the ice sheet and the melting on its surface (Levermann and Winkelmann, 2016). The ice sheet currently rises to an average height of around 3,000 metres into the atmosphere. Every mountaineer knows that the air gets thinner with increasing altitude and therefore colder. There are simply fewer molecules that can transfer energy to the thermometer, to our skin or to an ice sheet, and that makes it cold. Every kilometre upwards means a drop in temperature of around seven degrees.[8] Throughout the Holocene, i.e. for more than 10,000 years, the snowfall that gives the ice sheet mass was balanced by melting on the surface and the breaking off of icebergs on the fringes. As a result, the ice sheet was in a very stable equilibrium. Since the Industrial Revolution, however, we have been accumulating more and more carbon dioxide in the atmosphere, thereby warming it. We are slowly increasing the temperature of the air and water on and around Greenland. More ice is melting on the surface and flowing off as water. The ice sheet is losing mass, which is no longer fully compensated for by new snowfall, and so the sea level is rising worldwide. Critical to the tipping process, however, is the fact that the ice sheet is also losing height. As a result, its surface reaches warmer atmospheric layers, which causes even more ice to melt. Such a vicious cycle is called a positive feedback loop. So far in this book, we have called it self-amplification and will continue to do so. I would just like to briefly introduce the scientific term here. Please note that a positive feedback loop can lead to an increase but

---

[8] This so-called "lapse rate", i.e. the temperature drop per kilometer decline in height, varies with the humidity in the air and the atmospheric dynamics, but fluctuates around this value.

also to a reduction in something. The word "positive" only means that a change is increasingly reinforced. The system is therefore unstable. The opposite of this is negative feedback, where every change is countered by a system's reaction that reduces the change, i.e. every externally induced change is balanced out by the system's own dynamics. These systems are stable.

The moment the Greenland ice sheet passes its tipping point, a vicious cycle sets in: a self-reinforcing change that will only stop when the ice sheet has disappeared. At a certain warming point, self-amplification completely dominates the dynamics and the ice sheet melts incessantly, even if we stop warming the planet. The question of whether this point has already been passed is the subject of intense debate, and not only in the scientific literature. It looks as if this is already the case, and if not, then the further warming we will see in the coming decades will take us past this tipping point (Robinson *et al.*, 2012).

This example illustrates a number of characteristics of tipping processes that are useful to discuss. Firstly, the period of time until the tipping point is reached is completely different from the time span over which the tipping takes place. The Greenland ice sheet will take centuries or possibly millennia to melt completely. However, we have either already passed the tipping point or will do so in the next few decades. It is the moment when the original balance of ice loss and new snow has become so out of sync that the self-amplifying process of increasing ice loss has occurred.

The second very important possible property of tipping processes is irreversibility. In the specific case of Greenland, we could theoretically stop the tipping again and the ice sheet could grow again. To do this, we would have to reduce the temperature of the planet again in time, and then the ice sheet could recover. This is not the case for almost any other tipping point. As the melting process is so slow and is directly related to the temperature, this would theoretically be possible for Greenland. However, we are currently not able to remove carbon dioxide from the atmosphere to the extent that is even remotely sufficient to decrease the Earth's temperature again. This is a different discussion which would fill at least another chapter if not another book. At the moment there are no technologies that would allow us to take out enough carbon dioxide to significantly change the temperature of the planet.

Nevertheless, if we stopped just above the tipping point and the climate system could remove enough CO_2 from the atmosphere in time, or if we removed the greenhouse gases ourselves, then we could bring the ice sheet back into the safe range. But this is only possible if we stay close to the tipping point and act quickly. Many similar tipping processes, on the other hand, can no longer be reversed once the tipping point has been passed; they are irreversible. And from a certain point onwards, this also applies to the Greenland ice sheet. At the latest, when the ice has completely melted and turned to water, even a cooling of the climate would no longer be able to reverse this process.[9]

The West Antarctic Ice Sheet

The possibility of regeneration is a special feature of Greenland because the ice loss is so slow and we can theoretically intervene in the system by cooling. West Antarctica, on the other hand, is different. The positive feedback here results from an interplay of other processes: In contrast to Greenland, the ice sheet in West Antarctica is mainly grounded below sea level, not on an island above water like Greenland. Only it is so thick that it protrudes from the water far up into the atmosphere. Snow also falls on Antarctica and is compressed into ice, thus increasing the mass of the ice sheet. Unlike on Greenland, however, the temperatures here are so low that the gain in mass due to the snowfall is not compensated for by melting. Instead, the loss of ice, which has kept the system practically in equilibrium for thousands of years, occurs through the flow and sliding of frozen ice masses into the ocean. Antarctica is a large ice-cube machine, so to speak.

---

9 In physics, this is called a hysteresis behaviour.

The snow that falls on Antarctica is compressed into ice by its own weight and flows very slowly as ice towards the ocean. The further this solid block goes out to sea, the deeper the seabed on which it rests becomes. At some point, the ocean is so deep that the ice is no longer thick enough and loses contact with the ground. These virtual points that snake along the coast form the so-called grounding line, which plays a special role.

In West Antarctica and also in parts of East Antarctica, we have an additional peculiarity in the bottom topography. The seabed on which the ice sheet lies not only slopes down towards the sea, but also inland. The coast therefore largely consists of an underwater mountain ridge. The grounding line, where the ice begins to float up, is initially on the sea side of the ridge and is stable there. This has been the case for at least the last 100,000 years. However, this special geometry harbours a great risk. This has been known for a long time, but is only now becoming really relevant due to global warming.

When I was five years old, the British glaciologist John Mercer published an article in the scientific journal *Nature* in which he made a number of predictions about Antarctica (Mercer, 1978). First, almost 15 years before the first climate conference, he said that the Earth's carbon dioxide levels would double in the next fifty years if we continued to burn coal, oil and gas, as was already the case at the time. That was a simple extrapolation from observations, but it was a good prediction because it was close to the path we have actually taken. The next prediction was much less obvious. Mercer said that the warming this would cause would lead the ice shelves in the Antarctic Peninsula to shatter. And indeed, in 2002, almost a quarter of a century later, it was the Larsen B Ice Shelf that became the first ice shelf on Earth to make the front page of the *New York Times,* because it broke up into small pieces within 14 days. John Mercer's second correct prediction.

The real topic of the article, however, was the stability of West Antarctica. Mercer predicted that if warming melted the grounding line over the ridge, the West Antarctic ice flow would become self-amplifying and the entire West Antarctic would empty into the ocean. In 2014 – on a Monday in May – two publications appeared from two American research groups (Joughin *et al.*, 2014; Rignot *et al.*, 2014) that confirmed a French study from the previous month (Favier *et al.*, 2014). All three stated that West Antarctica has now become unstable in the Amundsen Sea. If these studies prove to be true, then exactly what Mercer predicted will happen (Feldmann and Levermann, 2015); sea levels worldwide will rise by more than three metres only due to West Antarctica (Bamber *et al.*, 2009).

I remember that Monday when the publications came out, because I stopped working and just looked at the wall in my office for half an hour. If this turns out to be true, it will be the first irreversible tipping point that we have actually triggered with our carbon burning, and it will change the face of the Earth. At that point, I had been researching the theoretical possibility of tipping points in the climate system for more than ten years. A lot changed for me that Monday. Dr. Mercer's work is a great example of the predictive power of physics. In 1978, he had neither computers nor satellite data at his disposal. He had only a physical understanding of ice dynamics, based on Newton's simple law,[10] and very sparse empirical estimates of the ground and ice topography.

If West Antarctica has become unstable, then, unlike Greenland, it can no longer recover even if the warming were to decrease. This is because, although the self-amplification process is caused by warming, the warming is not part of the vicious cycle that is responsible for the instability. The magnitude of ice flowing across the grounding line into the sea increases with the thickness of the ice at the grounding line. The reason for this is quite complicated, but you can imagine why: Even if the ice velocity did not change, the area over which ice is lost would increase if the ice thickness were greater. Because the sea floor in West Antarctica slopes inland, a retreat of the grounding line means that the ice sheet becomes thicker and thicker at the position of the

[10] The acceleration of a body is the quotient of the force acting on it divided by its mass. Known from school as $F = m \cdot a$.

grounding line. As a result, the ice sheet loses more and more ice, the more it has already lost – the vicious cycle is set in motion. As in Greenland, this process unfolds over a very long period of time. In this case, however, centuries rather than millennia.

The Gulf Stream and the North Atlantic Current

Most climatic tipping processes unfold on time scales that are much longer than our political, economic or social decision-making processes. The most famous tipping process is the abrupt cessation of the oceanic heat pump in the Atlantic. It is often referred to as the "collapse of the Gulf Stream." It would be better to say "North Atlantic Current," but it is actually a major overturning movement involving both currents. Relatively warm and very salty water masses flow northwards in the Atlantic in the upper 800 to 1,000 metres. Along the American East Coast, they are part of the Gulf Stream, then break away from the coast and flow as the North Atlantic Current across the ocean to Greenland and Scandinavia. There they release their heat into the atmosphere, become cold and heavy, sink into the depths and flow back south, where they become part of a complex global current system.

The self-amplification here is due to the fact that the North Atlantic Current carries the salt with it, which later, i.e. further north, causes it to sink. It is not only the cold that makes water heavy, but also salt. If the salt content of the seawater in the North Atlantic decreases for any reason, for example due to meltwater from Greenland, then the current becomes weaker, and the weaker it becomes, the less water sinks and the weaker the current in turn becomes: a self-amplification that can lead to an abrupt cessation.[11] If this were to happen, it would be like hitting the entire global climate system with a giant hammer. A catastrophic climate wave would sweep around the globe. First of all, the North Atlantic, including Europe, would cool down dramatically.

[11] As you might have noticed: In all tipping processes that we have discussed so far, it is the lack of something that self-amplifies. Less ice means more ice loss. Less flow yields a flow reduction. It's not just bunnies that can self-amplify, losses can too.

The heat that would be missing here would build up in the rest of the world. The sea level in the North Atlantic would rise by up to one metre. The change in currents would disrupt the marine ecosystem. The tropical rain belt in West Africa and the Amazon rainforest would shift by hundreds of kilometres, and weather systems around the world would be affected. Paleo data shows that changes in the North Atlantic Current have had an impact on the monsoon rain systems in both India and China.

Due to its enormous importance for the global climate, many great scientists have been studying the Gulf Stream system for decades, including the 2021 Nobel Prize winner in Physics Suki Manabe. However, the possibility of an abrupt termination of the current was first demonstrated by my colleague and mentor at the Potsdam Institute, Stefan Rahmstorf (Rahmstorf, 1996), who initiated decades of intensive global research on the topic.

3.4 What's Not Awaiting Us

There are a whole series of tipping elements in the climate system, and one could write a book on their dynamics, risks and consequences alone. In the context of this book, the key point is that they are another clear reason why the climate problem needs to be solved.

However, I would like to talk about a misconception that occasionally crops up in political debate. The global mean temperature itself is not a tipping element. There is therefore no warming threshold above which it becomes part of an unstoppable self-amplifying process. If that were the case, then the climate problem would threaten humanity's existence. It does not. The climate problem alone is not an existential threat to our species, as a nuclear war would be. If there was such a climate cliff, then behind this cliff the temperature would continue to rise until at some point, as on Venus, the oceans would evaporate and the greenhouse effect of the resulting water vapour would make the globe uninhabitable for plants, animals and humans. This will not happen.

Let me briefly explain why this is the case and why it is not controversial. To be clear: There are positive feedbacks in the climate system that cause global warming to lead to even more warming. A simple example, as mentioned above, is the sea-ice cover in the Arctic. The warmer we make the planet, the less ice covers the Arctic Ocean. As a result, less and less sunlight is reflected back into space from the white ice surface. Instead, the dark ocean that emerges underneath the melted ice absorbs most of the solar radiation, further warming the region and thus the planet. This process leads to additional warming, so it is a self-amplifying mechanism. The crucial point, however, is that it cannot dominate the dynamics of the Earth's energy balance, as would be necessary for the existence of a tipping process. The reason for this is that, in addition to the positive feedbacks, there is also a negative one that overrides everything and stabilizes the system, i.e. the global mean temperature. This stabilizing feedback is the so-called blackbody radiation, the thermal radiation of the Earth, which has already been mentioned above. It is at the beginning of every energy balance and is also central to the description of the greenhouse effect. The energy that a body radiates increases with its temperature.[12] This means that if we put more greenhouse gases into the atmosphere, then more of the Earth's radiation back into space is absorbed by the atmosphere and radiated back to Earth. The Earth reacts to this with an increase in temperature until, according to Planck's law of radiation, the energy radiation has increased so much that a new equilibrium is reached at a higher temperature. We call this increase in temperature global warming. It is the Earth's reaction to additional greenhouse gases and represents a so-called negative (or stabilizing) feedback loop.

The negative feedback caused by blackbody radiation is many times stronger than all the positive feedbacks that we have found or even

---

[12] The associated laws were found in the exciting period around 1900. In fact, Planck's law of radiation and the Stefan–Boltzmann law subsequently derived from it result from a fantastic combination of two of the three great theories that emerged during this period, quantum physics and thermodynamics. This can be seen very clearly in the so-called Stefan–Boltzmann constant: $\sigma = \frac{2\pi^5 k_b^4}{15h^3c^2}$, which combines Planck's constant h, the speed of light c and the Boltzmann constant k_b.

theoretically conceived of so far. The fact that it may take several decades for the new equilibrium to be established, because the ocean will continue to pump heat into the depths for a long time or the ice sheets will react relatively slowly, does not change the fact that this new equilibrium will be established.

This statement is recognized in climate research and is not controversial. Occasionally, however, words such as "unstoppable warming" are used in the media. This is either incorrect or refers to the delay in warming that we still have to expect. It is, however, essential for the climate debate that we do not have to worry about unstoppable warming building up. Warming will not become unstoppable due to a self-amplifying process that we can no longer halt. However, the Earth will continue to warm inexorably if we keep pumping more and more CO_2 into the atmosphere. We have the future in our hands – for better or for worse.

3.5 What's Awaiting Us

I do not want to speculate on whether the development of our civilizational over the last 10,000 years would have been possible without the climatic stability of the Holocene. In any case, it is a legitimate question, because agriculture emerged at the end of the Ice Age, and there is much to suggest that the climatic stability of the Holocene was and is an important prerequisite for the long-term development of our civilization.

The crucial question, however, is whether we can maintain our social achievements in the future. For over a hundred years, mankind has been burning carbon in the form of natural gas, oil and, above all, coal. These fossil-fuel deposits have been created over a period of tens of millions of years and have drawn carbon dioxide from the atmosphere in the process. You could say somewhat flippantly: It is the dinosaurs and their food that we are now digging up and burning. In doing so, we are driving the Earth into a hot state it has not been in since the dinosaurs.

Global warming is not a perpetually self-amplifying process; the Earth does not continue to heat up indefinitely on its own. But our growth processes cause the temperature to rise and rise – by about three degrees[13] for every doubling of CO_2 in the atmosphere. If we burn all the oil, gas and, above all, coal that we have found in the ground so far, we will make the Earth 15 degrees hotter.[14] This has consequences, not for our survival and certainly not for that of nature, but for our way of life. On the basis of thousands of pages of reports by the Intergovernmental Panel on Climate Change (IPCC WG1, 2021; IPCC WG2, 2022; IPCC WG3, 2022), which are based on tens of thousands of scientific papers, the international community has agreed that even three degrees more is too much – not for the Earth, but for us humans.

From the description of the tipping processes in Greenland, West Antarctica and the North Atlantic Current, it has already become clear that these consequences will be drastic. We live in a highly complex, globally connected world in which social relationships and their cultural traditions have developed over thousands of years. For our part of the world, democracy, the rule of law and the recognition of human rights are achievements that we can be proud of – many wars have been fought and enormous human suffering endured along the way. The big question posed by climate change is not the survival of our species, but whether our societies will remain stable and whether we can maintain and perhaps even advance their essential achievements.

The main problem of climate change with consequences for political conditions around the world is the intensification of extreme weather events. For twenty years, I have been asked in every interview on a flood, a storm or heatwaves whether they have been "caused by climate change." It is undoubtedly a relevant question, because it is *the question*

---

13 Whenever I refer to degrees with respect to temperature, I mean degrees Celsius. If you are used to the Fahrenheit scale, just multiply these numbers by 1.8 – or if you are lazy, double them.

14 The main emphasizes here is on coal, as coal reserves are many times larger than those of oil and gas. Coal reserves amount to around 2,600 gigatons of carbon, oil to around 450 gigatons and gas to around 350 gigatons, and this also includes so-called unconventional oil and gas resources (IPCC WG3, 2022).

of responsibility or, if you like, *the question of blame*. The corresponding scientific field is currently becoming increasingly important for legal claims for damages, as well as for the compensation claims of the global South in international climate negotiations. There are now sophisticated statistical methods for this so-called attribution of weather events to climate change, i.e. a scientific answer to the question of the extent to which climate change can be held responsible for the occurrence and severity of an event.

A different but at least as important question is how much weather extremes will increase in frequency and severity in the future. This question cannot be answered very well statistically, even if one is tempted to approach it that way. The reason for this is that mathematics provides clear and strict guidelines as to when a statistical trend is significant and therefore scientifically verifiable. As a result, science can only say unequivocally that a class of extreme weather events is occurring more frequently once the public has long since recognized this for itself. Only when something has occurred so often that every observer says, "Sure, it's happening more and more often now" do the statistical calculations sound the alarm.

A better way to approach the question is to understand the physical causalities. This now allows us to make very strong and reliable statements about the future development of weather extremes. Let's take tropical cyclones as an example. When they exceed a certain strength, they are called typhoons in Asia and hurricanes in America. It is difficult to predict how many of these tropical storms will occur in a season, as their formation is a complex physical process. The path that the storms take is determined by the local water and atmospheric properties. Even though computer simulations are improving rapidly, there are still very large uncertainties here. So we cannot predict how many hurricanes of what strength will occur next year and where they will pass through. This is just as impossible as predicting what the temperature will be next year on American Independence Day or German Unification Day and whether and how much it will rain.

But there is one thing we can say for sure: We know where hurricanes and typhoons get their energy from. The enormous energy that makes up the destructive power of hurricanes comes from the upper layers of the ocean. This layer not only has a much higher heat capacity than, for example, air or the ground, but unlike over land it can also be drawn from a depth of several hundred metres, simply because the sea is liquid. This has a simple but far-reaching consequence. If we increase the temperature of the Earth, we increase the temperature of the oceans and thus provide more energy for hurricanes. So they will become stronger.

This example illustrates very well why it is sometimes easier to make a relevant and robust statement about the future than a supposedly more obvious one about the past or present. The common question of whether climate change has caused this or that specific storm informs our desire to apportion blame. The more important question of whether such storms will become more frequent in the future informs us of the need to protect ourselves, adapt to the new situation and, above all, prevent worse things from happening. In many cases, the question of the future is easier to answer than the question of attribution.

The same applies to the increase in heavy rainfall events and flooding. First of all, more water evaporates from the oceans, rivers and lakes on a warmer planet. This water has to rain down again, which is why on average there is more rain on a warmer planet. Energy calculations show that around two percent more rain falls for every degree of global warming. This applies to globally average precipitation. However, the decisive factor for heavy precipitation events and thus for flooding is not how much water evaporates, but how much water the atmosphere can absorb and transport. This is why the maximum amount of water vapour in the atmosphere determines extreme precipitation. This quantity also increases with temperature. It follows the aforementioned law of the vapour-pressure curve by Clausius and Clapeyron from 1834 and thus increases exponentially by seven percent with every degree of warming. And the observed heavy precipitation events also increase by almost exactly these seven percent. This simple chain of reasoning is the reason why we should expect more extreme rainfall and therefore more flooding in a warming world.

Applying the Clausius–Clapeyron equation to the observed rainfall distribution allows us to estimate that the frequency of extreme rainfall events will even increase by 17% for every degree of warming. In 2023 the global mean temperature increase exceeded 1.5 degrees for the first time. The warming on land is about double the global mean. This means that the probability for flood events has increase already by 60%.[15]

In addition, global warming is shifting the temperature distribution and thus increasing the probability of heatwaves and droughts. Of course, this statement does not contradict the increase in heavy precipitation events, as there can be a flood in one place at one time, while there is a heatwave in another place at another time. The two can even alternate in the same place.

3.6 The Jetstream Concern

One of the most threatening causes of extreme weather events in Europe, North America and Asia is the jet stream. This is a wind belt that spans around the globe at mid-latitudes. Many of you might know it from the weather forecast, because it regularly brings us the weather systems in Central Europe. So if an area of high pressure brings us a sunny and cloudless sky for a few days in summer, then it was probably blown to us from the Atlantic by the jet stream. The same applies to an area of low pressure that brings the subsequent rain. The jet stream exists because the Earth rotates. It is part of the global wind pattern.

For more than 150 years, we have been observing the position of the jet stream to predict our weather patterns. Long before computer simulations helped with weather forecasting, the difference in pressure between the Azores high and the Icelandic low was determined by measuring stations in order to predict whether the jet stream would

[15] For the experts: $1.17^3 = 1.60$, which means an increase by $0.6 = 60\%$.

flow north towards Scandinavia or south to Turkey. Normally, the jet stream blows steadily from west to east, with cold and dry Arctic air to the north and warm and humid tropical air[16] to the south. The deviations from the normal position were important for weather forecasting, but they were usually relatively small.

Recently, however, enormous fluctuations in the wind band have been causing us more and more problems. One example of a whole series of dramatic events that can all be attributed to the meandering of the jet stream: In December 2017, the wind band in North America suddenly moved southwards. The previously warmer-than-usual winter in the north of the US was pierced by a cold front. The stream of cold air led to the condensation of water vapour in the atmosphere and covered the north of the US under a gigantic amount of snow. Social and economic life from Chicago to New York came to a virtual standstill for two weeks. An event that was repeated almost exactly one year later in a very similar way. Millions of people were affected, the economic consequences were immense and the media coverage was global.[17]

One month later, in January 2018, something happened that virtually nobody noticed, but was hardly less dramatic in its physical dimensions. In almost deserted areas of Siberia on the other side of the globe, the temperature shot up by 55 degrees Celsius in just five days. Here, the jet stream had suddenly moved northwards, bringing tropical air into previously freezing cold regions. If something similar had happened in Moscow, I suspect the hospitals would have been full of cardiovascular patients. But as it was, this seemingly fantastic event passed relatively uneventfully.

Another month later, in February 2018, it hit Europe. The jet stream moved south and brought minus ten degrees to Berlin. That's cold for February, but not unusual. What was unusual was that it was ten degrees

[16] The reason why cold air is usually dry and warm air is usually more humid is, of course, again related to the often-mentioned thermodynamic law of Clausius and Clapeyron. Warmer and therefore faster moving air molecules are able to supply more water with sufficient energy so that they remain water vapour and do not condense into water droplets – as described by the Boltzmann statistics.

[17] Most recently the same happened again in January 2026.

colder in Berlin than at the North Pole. The Arctic had not had seen sunlight for almost three months and should have been extremely cold. Instead, the jet stream had bulged so far north that this bulge tore off from the rest of the stream and moved around the Arctic as an independent vortex filled with warm air. This brought the North Pole, which was supposed to be around minus 20 to 30 degrees, to the melting point.

This sequence of events is part of a whole series of dramatic weather extremes caused by the meandering of the jet stream. Some still remember the Russian summer of 2010, when a week-long heatwave destroyed the wheat harvest and held the capital in its grip. The resulting peat fires could not be extinguished for weeks, and Moscow was partially evacuated. At the same time, floods in Pakistan temporarily created the largest freshwater lake in the world, displacing tens of millions of people. At the beginning of September 2020, the jet stream moved so far south through the USA that the Midwest experienced an unprecedented drop in temperature. In Denver, Colorado, the thermometers dropped by 34 degrees Celsius within 24 hours.

The Elbe floods in Germany in 2002 and 2013, and the heatwaves in Europe in 2002 and 2019 and in India in 2022 were all related to jet stream excursions. There is now at least one natural disaster practically every year that is the result of the jet stream behaving unusually.[18] By the time we have enough statistics to be able to say unequivocally that the meandering of the jet stream is intensified by climate change, such events will have happened so often that the realization will hardly surprise anyone. At the same time, the physics of the flow is complex and the scientific debate on this is still ongoing. The fact that the Arctic is warming twice as fast as the rest of the planet and mathematical derivations that this leads to a destabilization of the position of the

---

[18] There are two different effects associated with the jet stream, but I can only briefly touch on them here. A rapid slackening of the wind band leads to sudden changes in the weather. However, if the wind band has five, six or seven indentations on its way around the globe, a so-called quasi-resonance can occur. The weather pattern then stops, resulting in prolonged heat (as in Russia in 2010) or prolonged rain (as in Pakistan in 2010).

current are there (Petoukhov *et al.*, 2013), but there is no conclusive analysis.

It is clear that weather extremes have always existed. But it is also clear that climate change is making them stronger and more frequent. Overall, the assessment of the very cautious[19] Intergovernmental Panel on Climate Change is, with increasing vehemence and certainty, that the risk of extreme weather events will increase significantly with global warming, and in my opinion, this is a very mild and cautious formulation (IPCC *et al.*, 2012). Scientific predictions have never overestimated the problem. Reality has practically always exceeded the predictions.

The big question is what happens when the disasters follow each other so quickly and violently that we can no longer clean up in between. What would have happened if Hurricane Sandy had destroyed New York in the same summer that Hurricane Katrina hit New Orleans? What if the great drought of agricultural areas in the US Midwest had happened in the same year and snow disasters had hit the North the previous and following winter, as they did in 2017 and 2018? Where would the aid shipments have gone first? Would the Republicans and Democrats have been able to agree on a recovery plan, or would the world's oldest democracy have collapsed?

I would like to use this imaginary example to illustrate the real danger of climate change. The disasters described all occurred in the USA between 2005 and 2018, but there is no physical reason why they could not have all happened in the same year. Weather extremes are increasing at a rate that surprises even most climate scientists. And they are hitting societies that seem more fragile than one might expect eighty years after the Second World War.

---

[19] The Intergovernmental Panel on Climate Change, which is sometimes called the "World Climate Council" in Germany, reflects the consensus of climate science. This means that it mainly reports what all scientists agree on. Scientists do not like to agree. Science thrives on dissent, it thrives on finding out what nobody knows yet. It is therefore all the more remarkable that every five to seven years the entire climate science community is able to agree on more than 2,000 pages of scientific statements. That's how clear the state of knowledge is and has been for decades.

3.7 The Freedom of Our Children

In this chapter, I first explained how the temperature on Earth can be changed by the tilt of the Earth's axis and result in alternating ice ages and warm periods. I then explained why we are warming it by burning fossil fuels and emitting CO_2 into the atmosphere. Then, I used the examples of the ice sheets in Greenland and Antarctica, and the North Atlantic currents and the jet stream to describe some of the key systems that are responding to the man-made rise in temperature and causing the climate to lose its 10,000-year Holocene stability.

I have discussed extreme weather events to describe how the consequences that are already being felt will increase. If we continue to heat up our planet, we will probably not become extinct as a species, but the living conditions on Earth will change so much that we will be risking our political and social collapse. Migration movements, which are already a major challenge, will increase significantly as a result of extreme weather events. The flooding that led to the temporary formation of the largest freshwater lake in Pakistan in 2010 forced ten million people to flee their homes. We are also confronted with such events here in Europe, as, for example, the floods of the Ahr and Erft rivers in Germany have shown. In Europe we are already beginning to reorganize the water supply, which can no longer be taken for granted everywhere in the face of droughts and falling groundwater levels. These are all reasons why the global community now largely agrees that we must not allow the global mean temperature to rise by three degrees.

The climate problem is not an "eco problem," not merely a concern of idealistic environmentalist nutcases, nor is it primarily an environmental problem, even if we are experiencing dramatic changes in the world's ecosystems that are partly attributable to climate change. The climate problem is about the freedom and self-determination of our children, about their tangible material interests, which are absolutely legitimate, not least because essential achievements such as the rule of law and democracy are at stake. It is about the monstrous injustice against future generations that climate change represents. If the extreme weather events come crashing down on our society and our economy like fireworks, at some point we will no longer have time to clean up between the impacts. Then our rule of law and our democracy will come under increasing pressure.

This can already be observed regionally. The three years leading up to the outbreak of civil war in Syria, for example, were exceptional years of drought in the region. This illustrates how climate change will impact on our society. Not through one big wave that swipes everything away, but by ever increasing impacts and thereby exacerbating existing societal tensions which leads to civil war. The ensuing migration destabilizes neighbouring areas.

It can also affect us on a global scale: Colleagues from Columbia University in New York and the Potsdam Institute showed in a 2019 study (Kornhuber *et al.*, 2019) that the extreme weather events in the summer of 2018 were linked by a wave phenomenon in the jet stream. In a follow-up study in the journal *Nature Climate Change in* 2020, they were able to show that this phenomenon could affect all three of the world's main wheat-growing regions in the USA, Europe and Ukraine simultaneously with a synchronized drought (Kornhuber *et al.*, 2020). A so-called standing atmospheric wave would form, which would be held steady by the Rocky Mountains in such a way that it would hit all the world's breadbaskets at the same time. The same phenomenon, which already occurred in a milder form in the summer of 2018, only needs to occur with a little more intensity and the world's food supply would be in danger. As already happened in the summer of 2010,[20] in such a physical constellation the weather simply stops, and the synchronized droughts can last for many weeks.

The climate problem is destructive and incredibly serious. It is one of the greatest challenges of our time. It is not about the survival of mankind, but the preservation of our way of life. Climate change will

---

[20] This causes, as mentioned in the previous section, the simultaneous drought in Russia and flooding in Pakistan.

increase the pressure on our society in a way that at some point we will not be able to adapt to. If we do not solve this problem, the democratic constitutional states in Europe and America will eventually collapse, and hunger and poverty in the world will continue to spread. These are the dangers of climate change, and they are massive. Vegetation and fauna will outlast our intervention in the Earth's climate. The question is whether this also applies to our culture and our freedom. We are gambling away our children's future prospects of self-determination and quality of life.

3.8 The Climate Limit Is Zero

In the description of man-made climate change so far, I have ignored one important point: the question of what happens to CO_2 once it is in the atmosphere. How long do the effects described last? The answer is: much, much longer than our social decision-making processes (Figure 4). The CO_2 pollution lasts for generations. For all practical purposes, CO_2 stays in the atmosphere *forever.*

This has a far-reaching consequence: As long as we burn coal, oil or gas, the temperature of our planet will rise. If we do not mitigate carbon emissions, we will break the five-degree mark after a century, in the century after that it will be ten degrees and in the century after that we will have 15 degrees of warming if we burn all the coal we have found in the ground so far.

From this fact, we must draw a limit that, in my observation, has not yet been clearly understood in the public debate: No matter at what temperature level we want to stabilize our planet, whether at 1.5 degrees, as the global youth movement *Fridays for Future* demand and as agreed in the Paris Climate Agreement, or at 2 degrees, the absolute upper limit of the Paris Agreement, or even if we only want to stabilize it at 3, 4 or 5 degrees – no matter which warming limit we pick, we must go to zero emissions worldwide. The hard limit that the climate system imposes on us is zero. Because only with net-zero emissions will the temperature eventually stop rising.

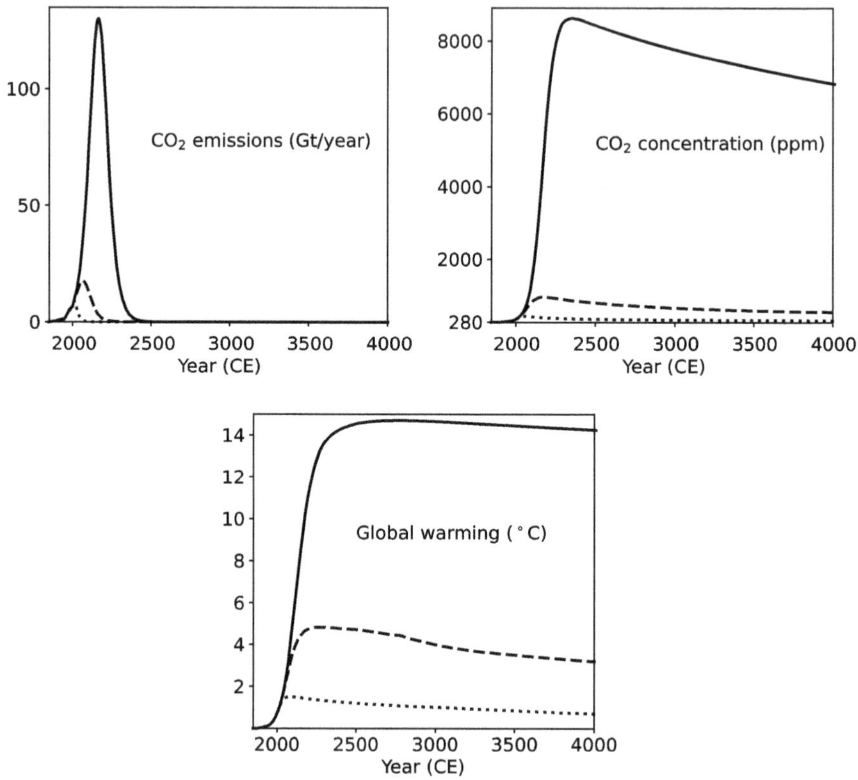

Figure 4. Response of the climate system to the emission of carbon dioxide with fossil carbon. Three scenarios are shown here as examples. In one, emissions are reduced so quickly that we still comply with the Paris Climate Agreement and stay below 1.5 degrees of global warming (dotted line). The second represents a world in which we do nothing to protect the climate in this century and only come to our senses in the next century, causing 5 degrees of global warming (dashed). In the third scenario, we burn all the coal, oil and gas reserves we have found, thereby warming our planet by 15 degrees. The following applies to all scenarios: Even after emissions have long since ceased (left), the carbon dioxide concentration only decreases slowly (right). The temperature falls even more slowly and, even in 2,000 years' time, is still at around the same level as at the end of emissions (bottom). Warming increases for as long as we burn fossil fuels and then remains practically constant. The consequence of this fact is that we must stop burning oil, gas and coal completely if we want to stabilize the temperature of our planet (Winkelmann et al., 2015).

The fundamental and comprehensive understanding of the greenhouse effect is what makes this basic insight of climate research so powerful and at the same time disturbing. We cannot negotiate with physics. It existed before we were here and will exist when we are no longer here. Of every triplet of carbon dioxide molecules we put into the atmosphere, one will dissolve in the oceans and acidify them.[21] This produces carbonic acid, which attacks the marine ecosystem at its base and is another major problem in itself. The other two molecule remain in the atmosphere for centuries as greenhouse gases and increase the temperature of the planet (Figure 4). The incontrovertible fact that emerges from this is that only if we completely stop burning fossil fuels can we stabilize the temperature of our home planet. This means that the solution is not to do less. The solution is to do something fundamentally different.

[21] The proportion of anthropogenic carbon dioxide dissolved in the ocean has fallen from 42 percent to 37 percent over the last few decades. One third is therefore a lower limit.

4 The Direction of Progress

> And for what? For a little bit of money. There is more
> to life than a little money, you know. Don't you know that?
> And here you are. And it's a beautiful day.
> *Frances McDormand as Marge Gunderson in "Fargo" (1996)*

Only if we stop burning fossil fuels will the warming of the climate be halted. Every additional emission of CO_2 causes a further intensification of the greenhouse effect and thus a further rise in temperature. Simply reducing emissions will not solve the problem, it will at best slow down the process. That's the first hard limit we come up against: zero. We have to get down to zero emissions as quickly as possible.

We already have enough experience with alternative energy sources to be able to say that zero emissions is a feasible task. Abandoning coal, oil and gas is technically and economically possible; it is the transition to renewable energies, and we are well on the way, just far too slowly. But climate change is not the only consequence of our industrialized, globalized way of life. It is leading to a whole series of other changes in environmental conditions that are no less serious in terms of scale and impact. I have already mentioned most of them in the context of planetary boundaries, such as the acidification of the oceans, the extinction of species and the consumption of resources. And because these problems are also well known, much of the public discussion on environmental problems revolves around the question of the weal and woe of our economic model, which is essentially based on the paradigm of perpetual growth. Continuous growth was and is linked both to a constantly growing hunger for energy and to the increasing consumption of resources: sand, water, land, rare earths. These resources are becoming scarcer, which the global community draws attention to every year by calculating for each country on which day of the year it has already used up the resources that are actually available. In Germany, the Earth Overshoot Day in 2022 and 2023 fell on May 4 – almost eight months before the end of the year. The frontrunners Qatar and Luxembourg had already used up their resources in February in previous years. Worldwide, the Earth Overshoot Day is currently in July, which is due to the significantly lower consumption levels in many countries of the Global South.

The overload days imply that there is such a thing as an acceptable, environmentally friendly level of resource consumption (just as many people still believe that climate change won't be so bad if we just don't emit quite so much CO_2). However, this only applies to resources that are renewable and not finite. For resources that are not renewable, we also come up against a hard limit here.

There is a fundamental problem behind concepts such as Earth Overshoot Day, an attitude that dominates many debates on environmental issues and which, in my opinion, is wrong: The dominant idea is that of "less," of restricting our current lifestyle, of some kind of material asceticism. A smaller ecological footprint is good, but too large a footprint is bad. Consuming as little as possible is fine. Those who drive less and travel by train instead of plane are committing venial sins. That is all kind of valid, but it does not help us on a societal level. Because where the hard limits emerge, where we have to get to zero sooner or later, reducing will not help us – at best it slows down the pace at which we are heading towards the certain cliffs.

Above all, however, I believe that the idea of reduction and austerity obscures our view of the actual task. We need to completely rethink a number of things; we need to change many things not just gradually, but structurally. This applies to energy sources, but also to the use of non-renewable resources.

Instead of arguing about ideologies of austerity or the demand that we must somehow return to nature, we need to think innovatively forwards, in the sense of a "third" industrial revolution, as proposed by the former director and founder of the Potsdam Institute, Hans

Joachim Schellnhuber (Schellnhuber, 2015). This also seems much more attractive to many and me. If we really rethink and find new ways to live our prosperity, this will also open up space for innovation and diversification.

It's harder to imagine this kind of innovation – by which I do not just mean technical innovation. Austerity seems easier to think about, and is somehow intellectually closer because it draws on something familiar; the "return to nature" has a long tradition dating back to Rousseau and German Romanticism. And of course, austerity is not wrong and is even important as long as we are still in the process of seeking and negotiating effective systemic solutions. But the idea of a third industrial revolution, a society that redefines and generates growth and prosperity on the basis of renewable energies – such a revolution would be a real transformation towards a sustainable future, which is much talked about but only spelled out by a few to this extent. In the following chapters, I will take a closer look at what these structural changes could look like.

Unlimited consumption of matter is not possible on a finite planet with finite natural resources. This fact has been emphasized and repeated so often that it has almost lost its punch, and the well-intentioned Earth Overshoot Day marketing campaign does nothing to change that.[1]

We seem to be racing more or less rigidly and immovably towards the hard limit – the day when certain finite resources will be used up. This is why we are increasingly hearing voices calling for degrowth, for growth to be halted. Given that current economic growth seems inextricably linked to increasing material and energy consumption, the question arises: Why don't we give up on economic growth? Why don't we try to get to a state of somewhat stable, unchanging conditions?

---

1 Frequently stating such truths without addressing the solution can lead to the realization receiving less and less attention. People settle into the realization without acting accordingly. This effect is greatly amplified by the speed of information flow in today's media world.

4.1 The Good Thing About Economic Growth

The idea of growth has shaped not only our economy, but also our lives and our social narrative for a very long time. Growth implies a promise – a promise of a better future. This promise is not only contained in the prosperity indices of gross domestic products, but also in a much broader sense in our idea of human history as one of constant progress. Growth means advancement, in society and for the individual. Our economy does not grow because someone calculates the gross domestic product and encourages us to push its value as high as possible. Growth arises from the drive and actions of people themselves, because growth holds the hope that a person's life will improve over time, that achievements will be made and goals achieved, and that prosperity and satisfaction will increase as a result. It implies the promise that the next generation, one's own children, will be better off than oneself. If I look back to the 1960s in Germany I cannot help but see how much our society has changed. Women play a very different role in our society now, men play a greater role in raising children in families, and we are freer than ever before in terms of religious, political and, above all, sexual self-determination. These advances are not necessarily linked to money, yet they are also linked to the increase in our material prosperity. We can now afford to take parental leave, pay for child care and have things delivered to our homes.

The growth narrative has long been one of the fundamental drivers of society and still is in many parts of the world. For many people, it is the reason why they get up in the morning, go to work and try to create something – for themselves, their loved ones and the next generation.

This incentive can be drawn from the macroeconomic perspective of the global economy all the way down to the motivation of the individual worker. If I get money from the bank to open a small business, this creates the incentive for me to earn more with my store than I have to pay in interest to the bank.

This is one of the reasons why many capitalist-minded people were concerned about the low-interest-rate policy that prevailed in Europe and the US for almost two decades. In the short term, low interest rates mean that you can get cheap loans from the bank with which you can build something. However, if interest rates are low in the long term, this means a loss of incentive for growth.

This aspect takes on an almost absurd flavour when viewed from the perspective of inflation. After all, a decline in value also generates an incentive. When money becomes worth less, people have to work harder to maintain their standard of living. In economic terms, inflation and interest rates are strongly linked, and a two percent increase in prices is seen as positive by many economists and politicians. If you translate this into the language of Lyapunov exponents – and a percentage increase or decline is exactly that, a Lyapunov exponent – it corresponds to a halving timescale of around fifty years. After fifty years, my money will only be worth around half as much as today. Here, as mentioned above, it is actually the loss that self-amplifies. I have to work powerfully against this negative self-amplification. If I want to pass on to my children what I received from my parents, then I have to work hard to counter inflation.

These thoughts are not new. But it is important to realize from time to time that growth has this important, undeniable meaning, that it creates incentives. Even without inflation: Growth is a promise of a better life.

The special thing about the promise of growth is that it has an effect in all areas of society and across all scales. It works at the level of the national budget of the Federal Republic of Germany and the US, right down to the smallest corners of the world. The idea of growth is not only so simple that it can be understood across all language barriers and many cultural boundaries. It is also linked in a very straightforward way to a system of rewards and punishments that seems to work in an almost cruel way for everyone: from the brokers on the New York Stock Exchange who make millions from nanosecond trading, to the employee who pays off her house and pays into her savings account, to the small

Indian farmer who has to earn food for his family from scratch every single day.

Growth and the associated incentive provide our societies with necessary goods, from food to clothing. I know of no comparable mechanism that manages with so little structure and is so widely applicable, because it is based on a self-amplifying process, which means that growth is robust and dominates its environment. All of this certainly contributes to the fact that the existing incentive system has been proven to work just as well in democracies as in dictatorships, and it seems to last long after large parts of society have broken down, for example in times of civil war.

Giving up this principle would not only require a great deal of courage. It would also only be morally justified if it was based on the firm conviction that something comparable could be put in its place. Something that works just as universally. Something that is just as easy to use and requires only minimal societal structures to operate.

There is another aspect. The desire for further development is not only important as the engine of an economic system and is not only a social necessity here. I am convinced that the idea of progress stems from a fundamental human characteristic. Our entire history shows that people have a strong inner drive for advancement, or at least for the feeling of advancement. There are many ways to feel this advancement, it drives us on long and short time scales.

On long time scales, advancement often means that we set ourselves goals that we work towards and eventually achieve, such as passing exams and advancing in our careers, as well as starting a family or building material wealth. The need for development can be satisfied by the constant acquisition of material goods, by rising in a social group, by raising one's own children or by acquiring knowledge and skills.

On shorter time scales, this need for motion manifests itself in other forms, but I believe it originates from the same aspiration. The lack of this short-term motion can also be called boredom. We often satisfy the need for short-term advancement through what we call entertainment. People were entertaining themselves with music and stories long before the electronic media world gave this aspect of our existence a completely different dimension, and the Roman emperors' motto that the people should be given "bread and games" also points to a very fundamental importance of entertainment in society. Entertainment gives us the feeling that something is happening without us having to do anything ourselves. It satisfies a basic need of our brain for a constant flow of information. Without external stimulation, we do not feel well, which is what makes solitary confinement so cruel and become torture after just a few days. Entertainment thus satisfies the need for motion on short time scales, just as economic growth and social progress satisfy this need on long time scales.

So on the one hand we have the social necessity of incessant advancement, which is potentially deeply rooted in us as a kind of fundamental desire, and on the other hand a finite planet, a finite space with finite resources. In many areas of society, development is not only identified as growth, but also as economic growth, which we in turn equate with the consumption of resources. This leads to a seemingly unresolvable dilemma. The resolution of this problem therefore begins with the question of what is actually growing when we talk about economic growth.

The gross domestic product is first and foremost a number. It reflects the value of goods and services that are turned over in a country or throughout the world. This value is a virtual value. It ultimately arises from a kind of negotiation process within society. People who deeply trust the market in which this negotiation process takes place are generally convinced that it produces the objectively correct price in some form or another, on the one hand for goods – i.e. matter – and on the other hand for services – i.e. the working time, innovative strength and energy that someone invests. A large number of studies have shown that there are many areas in which the market does not work – i.e. does not lead to a price that reflects supply and demand. This so-called market failure always occurs when the value of something is not correctly reflected by the market, i.e. the virtual negotiation process between supply and demand. For example, nurses in hospitals receive a much lower salary than real estate agents, even though their services are vital to society and there are too few of them. This is one example of market failure. But there are countless more. In cases of market failure, society must intervene.

Understanding the meaning of the term "value" in our society is essential for deciding whether we should adhere to the market economy and allow growth on a finite planet. The question of how value is created is not an academic one; it determines our life and survival on Earth. Despite all the examples of market failure, it is clear that the value of all goods and services is the result of a negotiation process. It is therefore both virtual and very tangible at the same time. Many people are convinced that material things, for example, have some form of "real value" and that there may be something added to this foundation of the real that arises from the interplay of supply and demand. Many consider this additional value to be unreal. Something like speculation is often associated with things acquiring a higher value than they actually have.

In reality, however, this foundation, the material value that seems to be taken for granted, does not exist. This realization is surprising for many, but it is important for the discussion about growth. And perhaps it would help to illustrate the whole thing with a few examples. If I had an unformed lump of steel, then it has a certain value on the world market. We would like to believe that it would have a certain value even without this market. But if a piece of steel was lying somewhere in the landscape[2] without anyone being bothered by it and without anyone having the tools and abilities to use the steel, then it would not have value. But if someone takes the lump and forms it into the shape of a container ship, the value of the steel increases many times over, even if no other material has been added. In the broadest sense, the new value has something to do with the labour and energy that went into the shaping process, but it is not simply calculated from the value of these additional costs that were incurred during processing.

---

2 It is clear that steel has to be processed to become steel and does not just lie around in the landscape. But this fact is not important for the argument here.

It results from what you can do with the new object, how much it is worth to society. You can quickly see this when you cut holes in the hull of a ship with additional labour and energy, thereby reducing the value rather than increasing it. You can argue for as long as you like about how much time and labour went into the ship – as long as it has holes in the hull, it is worth significantly less.

The whole thing becomes even more obvious with gold. For decades, if not centuries, gold has been the measure of wealth of people and countries. The gold reserves of the United States of America are stored in Fort Knox – well locked up and secured. The fact that they are stored there shows that they are not needed for anything. Hardly anything useful is made of gold. It is heavy and soft. It is neither magnetic nor does it have other impressive properties that make it necessary for mass production. Only relatively recently has it been used in the production of computers and cell phones. In the centuries before, gold had only two important properties: it shines and is rare. And that is why we have made it our currency. It has an almost completely virtual value.

The value of a thing is determined exclusively by a complex and non-rational negotiation process. As a result, the distribution of value in the world and between people is often unfair and irrational. However, this does not mean that this value is arbitrary, or even that we can negate it. We still need an incentive system that drives us to create value. Currently, this incentive system is leading to the destruction of our planet and uncontrollable climate change. But we determine what is valuable and what is not through our value system. If the Western world decides as one that Apple's iPhone is cooler than Samsung's smartphone, then more iPhones will be in demand and sold at a higher price. If they are produced in a different country than Samsung's, then more money flows into that country and the workers can feed their families and improve their lives.[3] The creation of subjective values objectively improves or worsens people's lives.

---

[3] As long as wages allow it. This is about the principle that subjective value decisions lead to very practical and tangible life changes.

As suffering and poverty in the world are far from over, we must continue to create value. We still need and will always need advancement; first, because we are constantly facing new challenges, and secondly to satisfy people's need for advancement: perpetual forward motion on a finite planet with finite resources. How is this supposed to work?

We face two major global challenges. We need the power that the self-amplification of economic growth ignites, but it must be decoupled from the destruction of our planet. A second, related issue is the fact that the self-amplification of economic growth is currently leading to insurmountable differences in people's starting conditions. We must limit both.

4.2 Ways to Limit Self-Amplification

I have argued that self-amplification can dominate the dynamics of systems and that it plays a destructive role for our planet through the consumption of resources. This raises the question of how to limit it. It is being asked so loudly because all attempts up to now are failing so spectacularly that they are threatening the very basis of our societies. Because one thing is clear: The explosive power of self-amplification processes cannot be tamed with gentle measures. It must be countered by similarly powerful processes.

There are various obvious mechanisms that prevent growth to infinity. All of them have their pitfalls. The most radical option is to stop the growth and thus eliminate the self-amplification process as such. This is the idea behind degrowth in general; it would involve changing the system. Given the fundamental importance of development for our society, I think this is a dangerous path to take, as we are simultaneously eliminating the incentive system. I am convinced that there are other ways to prevent planetary destruction, injustice and the disintegration of our society.

When it comes to population growth, however, this approach of fundamentally changing the dynamics is, in my opinion, the solution.

It cannot consist of a state limit on the number of children, like the Chinese one-child policy, because it is absurd to defend the preservation of our basic rights by giving them up.

The only morally justifiable democratic way out of a population spiral, which is currently being discussed and is already being pursued, is directly linked to the level of education and prosperity of societies. A number of studies indicate that a society in which women have free access to education grows less. And in fact there is no population growth in the countries with the highest levels of female education and prosperity. The reasons for this are certainly complex and possibly not universal. However, it seems important to me that this is a path that neither relies on paternalism nor contradicts the human, civil and freedom rights we have acquired over a long period of time. Increasing education and prosperity eliminates the growth process from within.

A second way of limiting self-amplifying growth is to limit resources. If there is not enough food for a growth process, then the growth and thus the self-amplification ends. If hares cannot find enough food, their reproduction is cruelly halted. The dynamic suffocates itself. This is how the tipping processes work: At some point, the Greenland ice sheet is simply gone, and the self-amplification process is over, because there is no more ice.

A third possibility is the competition of several self-amplification processes that keep each other in check. Famous examples are the so-called hunter–prey systems. The prey animals, let's take hares again, reproduce as long as they have enough food. If there are hunters that eat the prey animals, then their spread can be limited as long as the hunters find enough prey animals and also reproduce. Ideally, there is a balance between hunter and prey. In reality, of course, this situation is much more complicated, not least because there are more than two species, for example the regrowing food of the hares. Without human influence, the Amazon rainforest would probably end up in such a dynamic but stable state, with thousands and thousands of species stabilizing each other. Whether simple or complex, the principle remains the same – mutual competition can have a stabilizing effect.

A principle that is known to ecologists and economists alike. Unfortunately, these systems are not always stable and, above all, you cannot choose the equilibrium that is achieved. This naturally leads to a natural selection of species, and in both ecology and economics the question arises as to whether we want this.

What if you don't want to leave the field entirely to the principle of *survival of the fittest*? Then it gets complicated. Already the simple example of hares and hunters provides a number of important insights. First of all, the limitation of prey can only succeed if the hunters can reproduce. In other words, not only do the hares multiply through a self-amplification process, but the hunters also increase in number with similar force until there are enough hunters to eat enough hares. However, if, for example, only two male or two female wolves are allowed into a forest where hares can find practically unlimited food, the wolves will not be able to prevent the plague of hares. This is because two wolves will only eat a certain number of hares. Even if you let in an extra wolf of the same sex every year, you won't be able to limit the exponential growth of hares with a linear growth of wolves – unless you bring in an extremely high number of wolves, so many that you wipe out the hares. This analogy is enormously important for understanding growth processes. Among other things, it is the reason why our tax system fails at the task of limiting the financial differences in our society.

As long as you don't let exactly the right number of wolves into the forest to match the number of hares, there will either be a plague of hares or the hares will die out. This means that if you try to tame an exponentially growing system with a linear instrument, you need absolute control (i.e. the exact right number of wolves, unless they also multiply exponentially themselves and the "excess" wolves are then allowed to die). This way of controlling explosive growth requires a number of preconditions that are difficult to achieve in practical situations. The minimum requirements are a very precise understanding of the system and an uncompromising intervention that is neither disturbed by personal feelings ("Oh dear, the poor rabbits!") nor by corruption ("My son says he doesn't want me to let all these bad wolves in."). If you only counter a self-amplification process with linear measures, you are micromanaging instead of letting two processes balance themselves out. Our imaginary foresters have to be constantly vigilant and know every corner of the forest in order to keep the right number of wolves in the forest at any given moment so that the system does not tip in one direction or the other. This kind of micromanagement is complicated, and it puts all the responsibility in the hands of the manager.

This image is of course very simple – ecosystems, by contrast, are always complex. This becomes apparent, for example, when humans try to artificially restore the natural balance between hunters and prey. Usually the self-amplification processes then do not balance each other out, but lead to chaotic and unstable conditions. In fact, the hunter–prey models are among the first examples of the famous deterministic chaos that chaos theory deals with: Although the system follows deterministic, i.e. predictable, rules – and it would therefore be theoretically predictable – it exhibits chaotic, practically unpredictable behaviour. This is due to the fact that small uncertainties in the starting conditions of the system grow explosively due to self-amplification, making prediction impossible. Two systems that start almost identically are completely different after a short time. This makes them unpredictable and uncontrollable.[4]

Despite its simplicity, the image of the hunter–prey ecosystem can be easily transferred to economic mechanisms. Market economists hope that companies play precisely these roles of hunter and prey for each other, and that a market economy balance is established between them, an economic ecosystem that regulates itself. Politicians, on the other hand, are accused of only ever being able to micromanage with their instruments, pre-forms of a planned economy that stifle growth, disrupt the "natural" balance and thus achieve nothing.

---

4 For the professionals: Yes, there is so-called chaos control (I wrote my master's thesis in physics on this), but this requires a number of conditions that are not present in the practice of a real ecological or economic system with real plants, animals and humans.

In fact, what I call micromanagement is often a problem in politics because most policies are ineffective when they try to respond to a self-amplification process. To give an example: Of course, it seems sensible, as the French President Macron is calling for, to build a European Google. After all, the big tech companies in the USA fundamentally determine our lives in many areas, but are difficult for individual states or even the EU to regulate politically. However, Google's capital and market power have grown exponentially to such an extent that it is impossible to build something that could compete with Google. Even if gigantic resources were available. Google and Amazon grew in spaces where they had no competition and could develop without limits. The market power of tech companies is based above all on huge amounts of data that they have accumulated over decades and which now give them a lead in the development of artificial intelligence that others can no longer catch up with.

The fundamental problem with this third way of taming self-amplification, namely the competition of different self-amplification processes, is that you cannot shape the result. Instead of an equilibrium, chaotic or explosive growth of individual companies arises – consequences that we either do not expect or that we do not want. For example, you cannot simply add a "justice component" to such an ecosystem of self-amplification processes without fundamentally changing the mechanism.

All three of these options for controlling self-amplification growth – eliminating the process itself (e.g. degrowth), brutally ending a growth process that has nothing left to grow on (e.g. when there are no more resources) and competition between self-amplification processes that keep each other in check – do not seem particularly attractive for the reasons mentioned and many more. The question therefore arises as to whether it is actually possible to effectively limit the negative consequences of self-amplification that we do not want without undermining the process itself, i.e. without standing still or even going backwards. To put it another way: Is it possible to transform our growth, which is closely linked to destruction, into sustainable progress? This question can be answered in various ways.

We can continue to focus on growth and redefine what should grow. To return to the ping-pong ball from the prologue: The ball only defines forward flight as happiness, so at some point it happily crashes into an obstacle and shatters. The question is whether we succeed in redefining where "forward" is for us.

We can also continue to generate growth by creating material value without burning fossil fuels and without consuming new resources.

However, both directions are only partial aspects of a solution that must lie in the dynamics themselves. If we merely give unlimited growth a new sign (different values, less resource consumption), this does not solve the fundamental problem of self-amplifying growth. That is why I propose a change as a solution that lies in the growth dynamic itself: Folding.

5 The Concept of Folding

> I could be bounded in a nutshell and count myself
> a king of infinite space.
> *Prince Hamlet in Act 2 of William Shakespeare's "Hamlet" (c. 1599–1601)*

An adaptable being moving towards a danger will avoid it. If it is a wall, it will turn a corner to avoid hitting the wall. The being "folds" the path it is on in order to be able to continue moving. This is folding. It always occurs when a system strives for free motion in a limited space. The adaptation of the direction of movement enables infinite development in a limited space; it generates diversity in motion that would not arise without these limits. Thereby, folding produces solutions that would not be found without the boundaries. These are three characteristics that we as a society should take advantage of.

5.1 The Mathematical Idea of Folding

Folding comes from the theory of dynamical systems, a field of theoretical physics. To introduce you to it, I sent a table-tennis ball on a journey through the universe in the prologue of this book. I endowed this ball with feelings and wishes and then explained that the ball's luck lay in exactly one direction of flight: ahead. The ball, I explained, would prefer to always fly straight ahead, because its value system defines ahead as good and further ahead as better. It hardly needs explaining that this image, at least to some extent, describes our way of thinking about progress. In the Western world in particular, we have been used to seeing ourselves "ahead" for centuries, at the forefront of progress; and the spirit of "always further" and boundless conquest is still alive and well, and not just in the globally admired pioneers of Silicon Valley, above all Jeff Bezos and Elon Musk, who are in a space race with their rocket missions.

For the table-tennis ball, its characteristic of only defining "forward" as happiness is its downfall. Because at some point, the ball, which is always flying straight ahead, will reach a limit. It will pass planets whose gravitational pull deflects it, or at some point it will simply hit the boundary of the universe. The ping-pong ball will have to change its direction, and as happiness for the ball can only be found ahead, it will become sad.

To explain the folding, I then transformed the ping-pong ball into a golden snitch,[1] an active ball that is free to decide where it flies. Since its value system is fixed, this snitch will always return to the direction it originally took. Come what may. If the free-flying ball bounces against a planet, it will then turn back on course and continue in the direction of its happiness. It will do the same if it collides with another ball. As I explained in the prologue, this seems a little fanatical, but the ball becomes happier and happier. But again, his insistence on a single direction becomes a danger, at the latest when it gets too close to a sun and burns up.

The final, decisive addition – after I have first equipped the ball with feelings and desires and then with the freedom to decide for itself in which direction it flies – could be to give it the mental flexibility to decide in which direction happiness lies. This would presumably mean that the ping-pong ball would not just always fly straight ahead. For example, if it needed air to survive, it would certainly not leave the atmosphere. It would respect the limits imposed by its nature and its environment and stay close to the Earth. In other words, instead of stubbornly and rigidly insisting on one direction, the ball would adapt. It would no longer literally fly headlong into the wall, but would react to external circumstances beyond its control. And it would still manage to remain happy. That is the pivotal point in my story. Do we consider the ball to be unfree now that it doesn't leave the atmosphere? I believe it is no more unfree than a flock of birds that can move freely in the

[1] From the Harry Potter novels.

sky. It may not crash into the ocean or fly into empty space, but there is infinite freedom between these natural boundaries.

This is the folding. A system that constantly strives for something new and wants to grow as a result, but recognizes and accepts certain limits, will change direction and take a new path long before reaching the limits. In this way, the system explores the entire space within the set boundaries. It folds its paths again and again to avoid bumping into the boundaries.

Folding results from self-amplification in finite space.

Folding is the core of mathematical chaos research and was already intensively studied in physics thirty years ago. The findings of chaos theory, or rather the principles on which the theory of dynamic systems is based, and the knowledge gained from them have long since quietly found their way into our way of thinking. This also applies to quantum physics and the theory of relativity, even if not everyone is necessarily aware of this. Our view of the world is strongly influenced by our understanding of physics. The influence of chaos theory is, I think, perhaps the most significant since the ancient astronomers and scholars banished humans and the Earth from the centre of the universe. One example of this societal influence is the "safety through chaos" that we increasingly rely on in our modern day lives.

5.2 Security Through Chaos

In a very exciting way, chaos theory is not only the basis of folding, but practically the mathematical idea of our time. When I started studying it more than 25 years ago, I never expected this. Even more interestingly, a change in our society has prepared us excellently for adopting folding as a societal principle.

This was fundamentally different in my youth. Back then, the prevailing mindset of adults was characterized by the conviction that you could control things and events if you designed and executed them as precisely and perfectly as possible.[2] The world of technology and information was characterized by the pursuit of control and accuracy. A rather illustrative example of this thinking was the so-called Red Telephone. It was a permanent telephone connection between the two most powerful men in the world, the President of the United States in Washington and the General Secretary of the Soviet Union in Moscow. Even if the details of this connection were top secret, the basic idea is obvious: create a line of communication that is clear and simple and so well protected that no one can disturb or even destroy it. The well-founded hope was that the two people, who could have wiped out the entire human race through a pure misunderstanding, would not misunderstand each other.

Today, a single telephone connection on which the survival of humanity depends seems absurd, just as the Cold War as a whole seems absurd. We think that there must have been at least a second landline in case the other one broke down. And that was certainly the case. And then we think, maybe we should rather have a third one in the unlikely event that the first and second are broken or a terrorist organization attacks them. The idea that you create additional security with every additional connection that is independent of the others leads to the concept of the Internet.

Let's take this train of thought a little further. A telephone connection has many possible sources of error. First of all, it is relatively easy to avoid potential sources of interference. You can make the technical conditions so good that failure seems eliminated for any practical purposes. But then there are always those aspects that nobody has thought of, or those that are simply beyond human control. This could be an unfortunate chain of accidents or simply material damage that cannot be detected. The fact is that the security of a single telephone connection that reaches around the globe increases at most linearly with the effort you put into it. In fact, it is very likely that the closer you get to completely eliminating the risk, the more effort you have to put in, and that you can never guarantee complete security.

[2] Admittedly this conviction might have been particularly strong in Germany 😉, but I presume this was not bound merely to my country of punctuality and pedantry.

What happens when you calculate the risk of a catastrophe? You multiply the probability of the occurrence of a damage by the size of the damage. This works quite well when insurance companies want to calculate how much money they have to charge for their policies. You multiply the probability of a claim in one year[3] by the amount of the claim and get the lower limit of the value for which you have to sell the policy. But what happens if the loss is the death of everyone on Earth? How are you going to give this event a value that is not infinite? And what do you have to multiply infinity by to get a finite and therefore justifiable risk? The answer is: It must be a mighty zero. A zero that is at least as mighty as the infinity of the damage.[4] Unfortunately, in reality we can never get a zero on the probability side. If a failure does not contradict the basic laws of physics, then there is always a residual probability for its occurrence. Many argue therefore that events that would result in practically infinite damage should not be made possible. That seems quite reasonable but is another discussion for another time.

Now let us take the other path of risk avoidance. Instead of making one connection better and better, we simply rely on more connections. If the probability of one telephone connection failing is one tenth of one percent (0.1% = 0.001), then the second connection, if it is truly independent of the first one, reduces that probability to one ten-thousandth of one percent ($0.001 \times 0.001 = 0.000001$). A further connection even reduces the probability to one ten-millionth (0.000000001) of one percent. These are very small probabilities. But the really great thing is that the probability of a catastrophe decreases exponentially with the number of connections. So the idea that with a large number of connections you bring the probability of failure down to practically zero is a very good one, and because the probability decreases exponentially with each additional connection, it is a very

---

[3] It is actually the rate of occurrence, i.e. probability per time.

[4] In mathematics, not every "infinity" is the same. For example, the number of integers 1, 2, 3, 4 ... is infinite. However, it is less "mighty" (yes, that is exactly what it is called) than the number of all real numbers. These include not only all integers and all fractions, but also all irrational numbers, i.e. something like pi. Accordingly, a zero can also have different mightiness, because the reciprocal of infinity is zero. Mathematics is wonderful, isn't it?

mighty zero. The Internet takes this approach. An extensive network of connections on the World Wide Web stabilizes the connection lines between two points. You have thus reduced the risk of a connection failure to your own Internet access and the one you want to reach.

This type of solution requires a deep trust in chaos. Trust in the millions of different but opaque paths between the two points in the network. Not everyone finds this easy. Whereas we used to read a newspaper or watch *the News* to keep ourselves informed, many now rely on an almost erratic stream of information fed to them through social media. We no longer rely on the one newsroom that rummages through all the information and picks out the most important pieces for us. We rely on an opaque filtering process by the people we "follow" and algorithms whose programming we do not know.

I do not want to judge which is better, especially since I argued above that having a common information base is of great value to society. Instead, I just want to point out that we are slowly starting to trust chaos more than order. Because order can easily be upset. Chaos always stays the same. In this sense, chaos is more stable than order. A small change turns order into disorder, but chaos remains chaos, even if something is changed.

Something immediately becomes apparent: If we want to rely on chaos as a central principle of our society, then we need limitations. We need limits that protect us where it gets dangerous. I am convinced that even as freedom-loving people, we do not need to be afraid of such limits – on the contrary: Limits preserve freedom. If you set the right ones.

5.3 Folding Limits

Folding enables infinite growth in a finite space. That is why I believe it is the solution to our dilemma, which is that unlimited growth is currently creating problems that call our further advancement into question. It is not only the limits that are crucial and central to folding, but above all the freedom within these limits. Because infinite movement is possible within limited space.

Folding therefore allows something that is essential for us and will continue to be in the future: We must continue to develop as human beings. We are not at the end of the road in terms of shaping democracy, the rule of law and diversity, but are on a path, and this path does not have to be threatened by challenges such as the climate crisis and other environmental problems – on the contrary. If we set the right boundaries, new impetus and creative solutions can emerge.

Staying with the image of movement, we could say that instead of deciding between the two frequently discussed alternatives, upward movement (progress, growth) and movement in cycles ("back" to nature, degrowth), we consider a third: folded movement "forward," as growth and development that change direction when they reach their natural or moral boundaries. In mathematics, this describes a system that develops freely in a finite space, adapting to the limits of the space by avoiding explosion. It thus redirects growth where it explodes in order to turn away before colliding with the limits of the space. It is folding its path, its trajectory back into the space it came from in order to find new solutions. The more turns the movement takes, the more space it can conquer. Instead of unlimited growth in one direction, the result is growth into variety, into diversity.

The decisive factor, however, is that folding is not created by planning the trajectory. It is not a movement that is controlled step by step through micromanagement, but develops by itself by setting fixed boundaries. The difference can be explained using a simple concrete example. By micromanagement, I mean political decisions that aim to achieve a goal, such as reducing emissions, by setting out a precise path. For example, if the Ministry of Economic Affairs had passed a law stating that only certain heating systems could be built and not others. Instead, a limit in the sense of folding was proposed: In year *x*, no more heating systems that emit CO_2 may be installed. The type of heating technology we use to get there is left to the creativity and innovative power of engineers and entrepreneurs and the choice of users. A limit is set and the solution is entrusted to society. Of course, this only works if the limit itself is absolute and is not softened.

In the history of democratically constituted societies, there is a whole series of such fundamental boundaries, let's call them "folding limits," which have been functioning for an astonishingly long time.

The individual's right to private property is one of these limits – even if, as a "right," it does not look like a limit at first glance. When the right to private property came into being, it was declared that no matter how powerful a ruler is – he has no access to private property, no matter how powerless the owner of that property is. "Mine is mine," even if I am only a poor farmer with a goat and a few square metres of land. The king has no right to take it away from me or even enter it. This meant that the power of the ruler and the state over ordinary people was no longer unlimited.

The Declaration of Human Rights is a whole set of fundamental limits. It limited the power and arbitrariness of rulers even more. The universal human rights, which were proclaimed for the first time in 1776 in the Constitution of the United States of America and in 1789 during the French Revolution, limited the unlimited power of the mighty and were directed against the abuse of power and excessive force. With far-reaching consequences in all areas of life. The most visible example of this is the fact that the President of the US, (once) the most powerful man in the world, can neither influence nor revise a court ruling made in any of his states – as President, he is not authorized to intervene where the democratic system distributes power to others (this would not happen to Xi Jinping or Putin – because they do not accept such humanistically motivated restrictions on their power).

Or, to give another example of the consequences: In the course of the emergence of human rights and the associated right to human dignity, the penal system was increasingly freed from cruelty. Executions disappeared from the public eye, the death penalty was abolished in many countries and the penal system was increasingly geared towards punishment without relying on state intimidation – as is common in autocracies – and without allowing humiliation or even "revenge" in the form of excessive cruelty. If you look at how prisoners in, for example, Germany or other European countries – even murderers and rapists – are treated today compared to political prisoners in Russia or Belarus, you understand what an important boundary the Declaration of Human Rights has created. At their core, they mean that there are limits to what is permissible in the way people treat each other, that there is a dignity that must never be violated.

However, when human rights became the basis of democratic constitutions, societies were *de facto* still a long way from political conditions in which all members actually enjoyed equal rights. For example, the famous phrase in the preamble to the American Declaration of Independence *All men are created equal* did not even come close to meaning equal rights for all people, but only for privileged white men. Women and slaves were excluded. But the setting of this boundary has led to an ongoing process in which society has evolved in line with this folding limit. In the US, slavery was first abolished, then women's suffrage was introduced, and at some point segregation was overcome. And the struggle for truly equal opportunities and rights is still ongoing. The Declaration of Human Rights has thus defined a space with clear or sometimes still to be specified boundaries: no slavery, no child labour, no discrimination against minorities and the like. And our Western societies are still differentiating themselves within this space.

Constitutional limits can be visionary, oriented towards a distant future, as can be seen in the example of the American Declaration of Independence, which has been in effect for a good 250 years since 1776. The visionary aspiration also applies to the German constitution. Here, too, human rights were enshrined in the Basic Law in 1949, and yet it took until the 1970s before a woman could open a bank account in West Germany without her husband's permission, and even longer before homosexual relationships were no longer punishable by law.

The existence of such boundaries is only one necessary prerequisite for folding. Another is the constant progress of society, its incessant development. In finite space, this is only possible if the direction in which the system wants to develop is also constantly changing. This requires a perpetual adaptation of the value system.

5.4 Folding as an Adaptation of the Value System

Mathematics describes realities and, conversely, we can easily find examples in the reality of our lives to which descriptions from mathematics can be applied. Examples of "folded worlds" are science and art. In (western occidental) culture, each generation emancipates itself from the previous one by distinguishing their art from that of their parents and grandparents. This is almost always accompanied by an adaptation of values; the rules and norms that have emerged for the art of a particular time are questioned, changed or even discarded and replaced by new ones. What is considered "art" is renegotiated between the generations. Representatives of the older generation often consider the newly emerging forms of expression to be inferior – inferior to the old works. This is particularly evident in the emergence of so-called "light" entertainment. Comics, for example, were not considered art in their early days, just as jazz was rejected and the distinction between serious and light music, between the qualitatively demanding "serious" and the "shallower" light music, emerged in Germany in particular. But history shows that this is just as nonsensical as assuming that we are experiencing a constant increase in the quality of music simply because the new builds on the old. Mozart is not better than Bach and Miles Davis is not better than Mozart because they came later in history. They are different. And who today would deny Elvis Presley, the Beatles and the Rolling Stones or Metallica, Iron Maiden and Bob Marley their importance for our culture – even if they were classified as an inferior subculture, even to some extent as degeneracy, by the older generation in their day?

The image at the beginning of this book (Figure 1) is the result of a mathematical formulation of this idea. The line is created by advancing a point in the space of possibilities. The point can, for example, represent a currently predominant musical style of the young generation in the space of musical possibilities. The point here is not to claim that the space of musical possibilities is only three-dimensional. Three dimensions are just easy to illustrate. The decisive factor is the dynamics.

The point knows its own history and is always looking for a new place that is not yet occupied. In this attempt to distance itself from its own history, the dot constantly changes direction. In this case, the changes in direction are given by the avoidance of its own history, but only arise because the dynamics are limited in a finite space – in this case a sphere.

Some people may wonder why the space of musical possibilities should be limited. It helps to realize that limitation does not mean that the possibilities are finite. Limitation arise, for example, from the interval of frequencies that the human hear can hear and the rate at which we can distinguish different beats. Within these limits, however, there are an infinite number of possibilities for combining tunes and sounds. If space were not limited, the trajectory would simply disappear into infinity. This would allow it to fulfil its urge to explore uncharted territory, it would always move away from its own history without being restricted, but it would only move in one direction. It is only through limitation that diversity in motion arises. It is only through limitation that creativity and variation arise.

5.5 Folding Limits as Societal Visions

Folding limits do not inhibit freedom, but increases the incentive to create something new. In this respect, they are visionary boundaries. As such, they become part of a positive narrative that leads to a constant "amendment" of existing conditions. This is the progress for which the folding limit proves to be both an engine and a horizon. The old value system contains rules that contradict the new, visionary boundary – human rights, for example. The declaration of human rights, for example, has led to a long process of negotiation in which society has reformulated (and continues to reformulate) all those values and the associated laws, conventions and regulations that were not in harmony with human rights.

That is why today we take it for granted that physical violence and murder are forbidden – as is enslavement. But these self-evident societal agreements are part and parcel of a development. Thirty years ago, there was still a debate in Germany about "marital rape." In my youth, there was a large section of the population who believed that there could be no rape within a marriage because the man had a right to sexual satisfaction from his wife and she gave her consent when they got married. An idea that seems absurd to us today – because it is absurd. Other laws and conventions have disappeared. The discriminatory laws against same-sex love have remained on the statute books for an abstrusely long time, with the old value system shaped by centuries of tradition proving particularly stubborn. And although the legal regulations have now been adapted, social discrimination against homosexuals has still not been overcome. We have reoriented ourselves in light of the folding line and are still reorienting ourselves to it: human rights, the right to integrity and self-determination. Our world has become a better place. But we are not finished yet.

While old, no longer appropriate value systems are amended and renewed, completely new ones can develop at the same time. The emergence of environmental awareness has brought about particularly drastic changes. Rachel Carson's book *Silent Spring*, published in 1962, is regarded as the starting point for global environmental movements. Suddenly a wider public understood that scientific and technological progress not only brought blessings and unlimited possibilities, but also had a dark, destructive side. The book and the debate it triggered marked the beginning of social discourse, in the course of which knowledge about the finite nature of our planet became common sense, an integral part of public awareness.

When human rights were enshrined in democratic constitutions for the first time, they determined the further development of society – from the anti-slavery movement and the fight for workers' rights to the ongoing struggles for equal rights and social participation. Of course, the setting of these boundaries did not happen suddenly, but was itself the result of a long development, one of the stages of which was the philosophy of Enlightenment. These ideas developed over centuries and eventually became the subject of political theories (Locke, Hobbes) until they found their way into the constitutions of many states. I believe we have been in a similar process since the emergence of the first environmental movements. Rachel Carson's books and the Club of Rome report were followed by the emergence of "green" parties, the protests of Greenpeace were followed by the mega-demonstrations of *Fridays for Future*, in the context of which the decision of the German Federal Constitutional Court in spring 2021 was made, which for the first time in the history of the Federal Republic of Germany rejected a law due to its lack of effectiveness against climate change – almost sixty years after Carson's book.

These efforts to achieve a more sustainable lifestyle have long had an impact on our value system, which can be observed in many areas of society. For example, for many young people in Germany (yes, I am talking about the nation that loves its cars) today it is no longer important to have the biggest and fastest vehicle, but to get from one place to another as quickly and comfortably as possible.[5] This change may not seem very relevant at first, but it has a number of profound consequences. One need is linked to "having," the other to "being." If a pleasant and speedy journey is important to you, then sooner or later you will stop referring to the daily traffic jam on the way to work as the most individualistic form of transportation and instead argue for a generous and high-frequency rail system. Or our view of cars will change: What if it suddenly became prestigious to drive a car for a particularly long time? Whatever it may look like in concrete terms, the adaptation of values allows society to constantly improve within the framework of the current value system, because the term "better" itself is subject to development.

Today, more and more people, societies and countries can agree on certain basic convictions with regard to the environmental consequences of our actions. This is reflected not least in the 17 Sustainable Development Goals formulated by the United Nations, which have been in force since 2016. At the same time, we are still a long way from

---

[5] I am aware that we cannot speak of the new generation as a homogeneous group, and of course there are still people who would like to have a bigger and bigger car. I am exaggerating here in the hope that the reader will agree with my assessment.

finding satisfactory solutions to the rate of global warming and other problems such as species extinction or ocean acidification. I therefore believe that it is sensible and absolutely necessary to set new folding limits. This does not only apply to the environment. We can currently observe various self-amplification processes within our political and economic system, the explosion of which is not prevented by the existing folding limits and which therefore threaten our way of life. The human rights enshrined in the constitutions of many countries and our democratic state and legal systems continue to function and are not obsolete. But they alone are no longer sufficient to maintain the system, to limit a clearly defined space for prosperity, peace and growth. This is demonstrated not least by the fact that global crises are jeopardizing these very achievements. It is therefore necessary to contain certain self-amplification processes that characterize our present with a few new folding limits. Here I propose just five of these new folding limits which I believe would be sufficient to restructure our system and amend undesirable developments.[6]

5.6 The Best Search Engine in the World

During the Second World War, the United States of America gathered the world's brightest physicists to build an atomic bomb to defeat the Nazi regime and Germany's allies in the New Mexican desert. The list of brilliant minds who worked together in the *Manhattan Project* is breath-taking. This approach seems both obvious and effective. There was a problem that needed to be solved. So you bring together people who can solve it. Clear and simple. But the concept only works if you already know what the problem is.

Normally, research works differently. Just like a free society, free research usually chooses the tasks it has to solve itself. Of course, there is also knowledge generation commissioned by society and carried out

6 Without ruling out that others are necessary.

by scientists. Climate research, for example, receives funding to calculate the various future paths of climate evolution under different carbon emission scenarios or to investigate at what level of warming the West Antarctic ice sheet will tip over and discharge all its ice into the ocean. But the first step, for example recognizing that West Antarctica is potentially unstable, is done through the scientific search process,[7] not through government-funded "contract research."

This search process is the result of freedom coupled with the curiosity of the researchers. Scientists have an inherent drive to find new things. The fact that they create knowledge in the process is a nice side effect. That's why many of them continue to research even when they are retired or poorly paid. This drive needs nothing more than the freedom to pursue it. The limits are set by the laws of nature. This means that free research follows a folding dynamics. Creativity generated by a combination of drive and limits.

It is indeed a wonderful process and one that emerges naturally and has been moving humanity forward with extreme efficiency for thousands of years.

Society will do the same if you let it. The tougher the conditions, the more innovative the solutions. This becomes very clear in the inhospitable regions of the world that humanity has penetrated. People live in the Arctic in areas that are far too cold for their body temperature and that provide little vitamin-rich food. The hard limits imposed by human physiology have set creative and innovative forces in motion, as demonstrated, for example, by the Inuit and desert cultures around the world. These are examples of solutions that have developed over long time scales. But the same applies, of course, to inventiveness during catastrophes such as wars or natural disasters. The rescue of the British

---

7 The possibility of West Antarctic instability, for example, was recognized by glaciologists fifty years ago (Mercer, 1978; Weertman, 1974). At that time, the assignment given by society to scientists was not to find the greatest risks from global warming, but simply to understand our world. Truly new things are generally not created through commissioned research, but through free research. Because it is not the funders who know where to look for the exciting findings, but the scientists.

soldiers from Dunkirk during the Second World War is one of these solutions that lay way outside the normal strategies of the military.[8]

The fact that we do not like to stagnate, but feel the urge to constantly develop further, makes us as a society a permanent source of innovation and renewal. If this process of discovery is not restricted, i.e. if new solutions can constantly emerge in a society that operates freely within certain limits, society's urge to move and innovate becomes a powerful search engine.

In this sense, folding is the opposite of a planned strategy. In the same way, it is the opposite of a command economy.[9] Finding a planned solution may seem more reassuring because, in addition to the goal, large parts of the path are also predetermined. However, the planned solution can only be as clever as the planner. Finding a solution by folding can be much smarter than a single person. Free, unplanned, chaotic research into solutions works so well because it is ergodic.

The concept of ergodicity comes from physics, and it explains why folding, as a system of maximum freedom and minimum necessary control within a few hard limits, is such a powerful search engine. A system is ergodic if it occupies every possible state that it can assume within the limits set by the laws of physics. Imagine a dog that is sitting in its kennel and sees its owner coming around the corner. It immediately jumps up and runs in a straight line towards its beloved caregiver. It could also explore the world and get to know new people or even meet other dogs, but it does not do that because it is a command-economy dog. It has a goal and strives towards it in a straight line.

Now imagine an ant. It wanders through the world looking for food for the tribe. It does not know where to find food and seems to wander aimlessly. However, it actually has a goal and as soon as it senses an

---

[8] Around 500,000 British soldiers were encircled by the German Wehrmacht in Dunkirk. The British fleet was held in check by the German air force and was unable to help. In the end, the soldiers were heroically rescued by an improvised fleet of private boats.

[9] Or "planned economy," as there was in the Soviet Union or the Eastern German Democratic Republic.

indication of food, it turns in that direction. This search is not entirely random. It is influenced by various aspects of the environment, and also by the search of the other ants. As a result, the ant colony explores the entire environment and also repeatedly finds new sources of food, such as the cheese sandwich that my child left out in the sun. The ants' search is ergodic. It is strictly limited by the radius of an ant's walking distance from its formicary, but by nothing else.

5.7 The Solution to the Dilemma

Folding offers the opportunity to avoid conflicts with the limits we are naturally given, to set ourselves ethical and moral boundaries and to develop freely within them. It is also the principle of choice when it comes to finding new problems and finding genuinely new solutions to them.

Of course, this does not mean completely abandoning the planned-solution-finding method. The planned solution is the method of choice when you know the problem and can already anticipate the solution; and, of course, planning is a necessary part of our everyday lives. That remains true despite the fact that our daily use of the Internet has brought us emotionally closer to ergodic problem solving. Ergodic search is less predictable, but much more stable and accurate if you have the nerve for it. Society's search for new paths within newly emerging physical or moral boundaries should proceed according to the principle of folding, i.e. ergodically. It is the liberal-democratic way to search for something new.

A very hard condition, however, is that the folding boundaries are fixed and cannot be circumvented. Within these folding limits, all other boundaries and rules can be constantly adapted in a social process of change. This must be done openly and transparently and must not be defrauded by corruption or backroom deals. Limiting carbon dioxide emissions is a good example of this. Even in the middle of the last century, it was not yet clear to society that additional carbon dioxide in the atmosphere would be a problem, although the physical theory already existed and was well established.[10] In the meantime, we have learned, the theory became certainty decades ago, and a societal process (that has been far too slow and painful for many of us) has been set in motion. Now we are in the process of introducing a new folding limit, and this new limit has already generated innovation, and will continue to do so – as I will outline in Chapter 6. It is absolutely crucial that the freedom that we have within this new folding limit is not being exploited to delay the process of change. The call for open-mindedness with respect to the specific technological solutions to the climate problem has been used in the past by people who wanted to ignore the limit and delay the process. This is extremely dangerous and delays or even inhibits the solution. Even though it is often stated otherwise, it slows down innovation if you soften the folding limit because you allow people and companies to continue on an old path that they will eventually have to leave. It is like allowing your little kids to use the iPad in order to get some peace and quiet. As understandable as that is, it is not good for them and eventually they will have to give it up and face life outside the Internet.

Another important aspect of the folding principle applied to society is that new boundaries not only lead to innovation in technologies but also yield an adjustment of our value system. As in the theory of dynamic systems, the system realigns its coordinate system and seeks new paths without perceiving them as a restriction of freedom. The reason is that there is always infinite room for change and development.

Sometimes you dynamically pass similar places several times – even without having introduced new boundaries. These places are never exactly the same, and that is precisely why their passing constitutes an advancement. For example, it was once acceptable in many parts of the world to have chores done by people who had no rights and were considered serfs. At different times in different countries, we

[10] The physical connection between carbon dioxide and global warming has been known for much longer. The Scandinavian Nobel Prize winner Svante Arrhenius published on the role of greenhouse gases, particularly carbon dioxide, at the end of the 19th century. He was also the first to estimate the above-mentioned climate sensitivity, i.e. the warming that results from a doubling of CO_2 in the atmosphere.

have agreed on the boundary that no human being can belong to another. We implemented that for mainly ethical reasons despite the fact that it was economically unfavourable for the wealthy part of society. These wealthy people in many parts of the world then switched to a domestic servant system, in which employees were theoretically free, but in practice still bound to "their masters." Again, boundaries were drawn to break down this dependency, which worked more or less well and more or less quickly. As a consequence, in most Western democracies today, we have laws that no longer tolerate slave-like employment.

In many Western societies (and of course not only there), women had taken on or were given the domestic work. This has been facilitated and promoted by a very old narrative that says housework is a woman's natural task. As absurd as this idea is, it is alive and thriving in many European countries and the US again. Advances in technology allowed housewives to take on jobs that previously required multiple domestic workers. This narrative that relegates women to the stove is slowly being replaced, and the question is: What comes next? After all, household tasks have not disappeared as a result of technological progress; housework is a necessary and meaningful activity. It is therefore possible that we are experiencing a transition to a new system in which housework, care work and, to a certain extent, parenting are transitioned more and more to paid and outsourced labour.

The examples show that we are constantly changing and adapting our value system under the implementation of a set of folding limits. In this case these folding limits are the Human Rights. The idea that all humans have equal rights. The adaptation of our value system is an absolutely necessary dynamic in order to identify and eliminate errors and injustices. In many cases, it takes an unbearably long time and we are constantly experiencing setbacks, and progress is way too slow. This does not change the fact that this social dynamic is a powerful motor for development and progress, not *despite* certain limits, but precisely *because* these limits exist, as a framework that allows the greatest possible freedom within these limits.

It is becoming increasingly clear that we need to place new limits on certain exploding, self-amplifying processes in order to prevent our societies and the Earth on which we live from being torn apart. These new limits must not excessively restrict our freedom, and should avoid small-scale regulation as in a planned economy. We need certain new boundaries that will counteract dangerous self-amplification processes in order to hold our societies together. The exact implementation of the principle of folding is of course a matter for discussion. The decisive factors are the reliability and steadiness of the boundaries and the simplicity and transparency of the rules so that they can be supported by society.

Just like equality before the law and in voting, we must accept the finite nature of our planet and its resources and reconcile this with our basic need for development. Folding is the solution to this supposed dilemma. We need an economic system that grows due to limits, because this is the only way to generate the creativity we need to solve future challenges.

5.8 Folding as an Economic Principle and Raison d'État

Growth into diversity is a very hard principle. It stabilizes the internet and ecosystems. Biodiversity is a cornerstone of the natural adaptability of ecosystems to external and internal changes. The Internet was invented to create the most stable communication links between two points. As mentioned above, the multitude of connections makes it much more stable than a single connection – no matter how well-protected this single line might be. And diversity is also the solution of choice in business. New things are constantly being created to keep demand high and the economic world moving. It is therefore a truly ubiquitous principle. It unleashes competition and a spirit of innovation.

However, one component in our economic system is currently still wrong and hinders both competition and sustainability, and that is the absence of limits. We must continue to allow a market economy to thrive in the future and with it the entire range of achievements of a liberal democratic society. What must be prevented is individual growth into *de facto* infinity, the breaking of our planetary boundaries, the exhaustion of our global common goods. As already described, we are already setting limits to our actions today, namely where we consider them ethically necessary. Slavery, child labour and the trade of radioactive materials are just a few examples.

In the meantime, however, it is becoming clear that our existing limits are no longer sufficient. This is because the original promise of economic growth, that future generations should be better off than us, is currently being turned into its opposite by precisely this economic growth – because at the moment unlimited economic growth goes hand in hand with environmental destruction and, among other things, causes climate change, which fundamentally threatens our way of life.

We have to accept the finite nature of our planet as an additional limit. This extends beyond climate change of course. For example, plastic is a man-made product that will outlive every human being. We now find microplastic in the most remote areas of the Earth. On every beach in the world, whether it has ever been walked on by a human or not, microplastic is mixed into the sand. The snowfall on Greenland and even on Antarctica contains microplastics.[11] A plastic ban, which is slowly being introduced in various countries and economic sectors, is generating alternative packaging and alternative ways of consumption. The crucial aspect of this dynamics is that the solutions are not prescribed, but merely the limits that the system must not exceed are set. This is the opposite of a planned economy. It is a free economy within strictly set limits.

---

11 Antarctica is the only continent on Earth that can only be accessed by researchers. It is huge – the size of North America from Mexico to Canada – and following the 1959 Antarctic Treaty, no one is allowed to go there unless this person is exploring the region for the benefit of mankind. Physically, Antarctica is shielded from the rest of the world by the largest ocean current on Earth and the most powerful atmospheric vortex on the planet. And still, on the coasts of this remote continent, microplastics fall within the fresh snow.

This means that we also need a new kind of politics. A large majority of society agrees on goals, such as sustainability. No one in their right mind can be in favour of the extinction of other species. The arguments that hold us back are related to "side-effects" of sustainability. The problems are made complicated and we are convinced that sustainability cannot be achieved unless we completely change our lives.[12] In reality the path to sustainability is complicated in detail, but not in principle. We will only make progress in finding solutions if we once again have the courage to entrust them to society to a considerable extent, instead of setting small-scale political guidelines and thus engaging in micromanagement. In order to unleash the necessary creative power, we need certain boundaries – the folding limits. They are absolutely necessary to stop dangerous developments. But we also need the courage to rely on the creativity and innovative power of society in the search for new, folded paths instead of small-scale, sometimes short-sighted guidelines "from above." The question is whether we are politically and socially prepared to set a few new, hard folding limits. Underlying is the question: Do we understand adaptation in the future exclusively as an unavoidable reaction to increasingly painful disasters – as we recently experienced ourselves, for example, in Germany with the floods on the Ahr and Erft rivers – or do we create a creative, forward-looking adaptation that we control and shape ourselves by setting the necessary limits?

If we assume that the paradigm of progress, or at least the paradigm of constant motion and change, cannot be dissolved, i.e. that society is constantly striving for advancement and improvement, then the question is how we can direct these forces constructively. The neoclassical economic answer to this question is economic growth. Above, I have already described economic growth as a system of incentives. In conjunction with democracy and the rule of law, one of the advantages of this system is that it makes every single member of society responsible. The promise of progress implies that it is worth

[12] Interestingly this is done by both sides – people who want to achieve sustainability and those who just want to stall and are actually in favour of keeping everything as it is.

making a constructive contribution to shaping society. This encourages large sections of society to actively participate in shaping all areas of life. Doing without this engine seems dangerous and absurd to me; I also do not believe that we could even estimate what the consequences would be if we eliminated this incentive structure.

As a driver of development, economic growth has functioned across all scales and systems for centuries and has led to constantly increasing prosperity worldwide. Yet it has its undisputed downsides. And these are increasingly overpowering and destroying its upsides. One problem with economic growth is that it has a one-dimensional metric. There is only "more" or "less." This metric is too simplistic for the complexity of our society. We use a system where we map everything we want onto this one-dimensional metric. Many people who criticize the concept of money are essentially referring to this fact.

Money-based trade provides us with an important motivation in society for constructive and targeted work. But at the same time, we should make sure that money does not dominate our entire value system. The reason is simple: We cannot map all our needs onto a one-dimensional metric. It is difficult to decide whether Christmas with the family is worth 100 euros or 1,000 or priceless. Even with absolutely necessary activities, it is not the case in today's system that we always act solely on the basis of financial incentives. A nurse or doctor does not work on Christmas Eve because there is more money, but because it is their job and this job also includes weekend and holiday duties. The motivation is nourished by a narrative that led them to choose these idealistic professions.

If we introduce limits in a constantly advancing system and those affected know about the limits, then they will align their efforts accordingly as long as they accept the limits as fixed. In other words, if a company can safely assume that in twenty years' time it will not be allowed to emit any carbon dioxide during production, then it will find a way to make a profit without carbon dioxide by then. It will get creative and change direction or its value system, namely the definition of what is good and bad for the company.

The same applies to individuals. The majority of people in my parents' generation defined success by how big a car they could drive. That might be a German thing, but I guess we can find similar examples everywhere. In Germany right now, there is an incredible shift happening in large sections of society, whereby massive cars are something to be ashamed of. In this case, the change did not occur in response to a limit that was set, but that would have been a possibility. Instead, this car revolution has come about due to a combination of factors. First, a conviction has slowly spread that driving is bad for the environment and the climate. The *Fridays for Future* movement has clearly addressed the conflict on behalf of the younger generation and made drivers of combustion engines understand: You are driving against your children's future. But for a long time, there was no viable alternative. Then Tesla showed that electric cars could be such an alternative, and within a very short time, all the other car companies that had resisted this technology for decades with intense lobbying brought electric cars onto the market. Finally, the European Union set a target date for banning the registration of new combustion engines to the year 2035. The fact that so many companies have brought electric cars onto the market in such a short period of time shows that technology was not the problem. Surely this revolution would have been possible much earlier if we as a society had set a date beyond which combustion engines could no longer be sold.

If we accept the narrative of folding as an economic principle and raison d'état, then it should be possible to draw such limits politically and thus direct the innovative power of the economy towards the future we want as a society. If we succeed in doing this, we will reclaim the space for the social and political forging of our future instead of letting the economy and technology dictate the direction we move to. We can achieve this with the democratic institutions that already exist. We just need to reform their functions: no more fear of bans, but at the same time no micromanagement. And I'll say it again because it is so important: We need the creative freedom of the economy. We should only ban explicitly the things that we do not want. Maximum freedom must be allowed within these limits.

The prohibitions we set must be absolute, they must constitute folding limits. This means that they no longer need to be compromised once we have decided to set them in a political process. This lack of compromise in political decisions sounds inconceivable at first, because at the moment all political processes happen as compromises. However, the limits I am referring to are so absolute that they do not require compromise. The prohibition of slavery requires no compromise. It is absolute. Just like the ban on carbon dioxide emissions.[13] The number of new folding limits that we have to draw is quite small and they are quite simple. I will discuss five additional folding limits in the upcoming chapters of this book.

Once a new boundary has been established, the real work begins. Because then it becomes clear that a great deal of effort and restructuring is required to comply with it. During this process, many will curse the limits and wish they had never been introduced. But little by little, the system changes and society finds new ways. Until the limits we have set seem completely natural to us, just as no sensible entrepreneur in Europe or the US today, for example, ever thinks about how good it would be for their business to reintroduce slavery. The limit, once a vision, has become part of our value system (the fact that forms of modern slavery exist is not an objection, but a reason to constantly strive to combat such abuses – which is also happening in Europe through regulatory projects such as the Supply Chain Act). In the same way, we could define "good textiles" in the future not just as "cheap, high-quality clothing," but as "affordable, good clothing with fair working conditions and acceptable environmental standards." At some point, we will no longer even have to think about it, because all the clothes we can buy will meet the additional condition that they were produced under humane conditions.

---

[13] As explained in Chapter 3, the temperature of the planet will continue to rise as long as we burn oil, gas and coal, because the fossil carbon remains in the atmosphere for hundreds to thousands of years.

The folding limits that I am proposing would be a necessary first step in this direction. Similar to the emergence of democratic constitutions, they could represent a beginning, a vision that clarifies the goals towards which the innovative power in our society will be directed in the future.

To demand that every individual introduces new limits every day for a long period of time while the society around them does not is asking too much. But if we are convinced that a certain limit is actually necessary, then we can introduce it as a society and use the innovative power of individuals and the economy to find the best possible way to live with this limit. The limit is then not perceived as a restriction of freedom, but as an incentive for innovation. Just as the ecological diversity in the Amazon rainforest is only created by its limited space and availability of resources. The forest cannot simply expand. The plants and animals compete within the natural boundaries and have developed into a quasi-infinite biodiversity.

Growth into diversity not superiority is the constructive way of progress without loss of incentive.

6 Folding Production: Limits and Innovation

> Life is sustainable now! ... I don't want to survive.
> I wanna live.
> *Captain B McCrea in "WALL-E" (2008)*

Can the principle of folding really be more than just a nice mathematical description of existing ideas? It becomes interesting when we place it alongside our other basic social principles. When we accept limits – such as the finite nature of our resources and common goods – as the incontrovertible truth that they are. In the case of climate change, this irrefutability arises from the physics of our atmosphere and oceans, and from the chemistry and biology of our planet's carbon cycle. The challenge this poses is huge. But we can overcome it.

Folding can be the answer not only to this, but also to a number of major challenges of our time, including the climate crisis and the much broader problem of sustainability and the associated loss of biodiversity.

6.1 The Climate Limit: No More Fossil Carbon

The solution to the climate problem is to stop burning fossil carbon, i.e. oil, natural gas and coal. And unfortunately, this is non-negotiable for a number of tangible reasons.

Just as there are people who fear that if we exceed a certain point of warming, we will enter an infinite spiral of global warming and thus drive humanity to extinction – an unfounded concern[1] – there are also people who believe that the climate problem will dissolve itself.

[1] The explanation as to why we need not fear such a spiral on Earth was given in Chapter 3.

Unfortunately, this hope is even less well-founded. It is often nourished by ignorance or the conviction that humanity is ultimately too insignificant and would not be able to bring about a truly global natural catastrophe unless it waged a worldwide nuclear war. The climate, so the trivializers hope, will regulate itself and return to its former state after a period of adaptation. Unfortunately, this is not the case. The climate will not recover from our influence, at least not in the foreseeable future, for hard physical reasons.

Here again, the time scales are of crucial importance. They determine qualitative differences, although they describe a quantity. It is a fundamental and therefore qualitative difference whether carbon dioxide remains in the atmosphere for 50 or 500 years. If it were 50, then the whole thing would be a problem for the generations living today – parents and their children. It would be tangible and negotiable.

Figure 4 shows how slowly additional carbon dioxide, once released into the atmosphere, disappears again. Long after emissions stop, most of the CO_2 is still in the air. The temperature drops even more slowly. This is because the ocean is warming up and is only slowly releasing the heat back into the atmosphere after carbon dioxide levels drop. The ocean acts as an energy buffer, basically a heat bath for the entire planet.

The enormity of the time span over which this unfolds is again difficult to grasp. You can try by imagining what our society was like around the year 1500 CE.[2] Or you can try to understand it by realizing that you do not know anyone who knew someone who lived through that time from the Middle Ages till today. In the same way, almost all of us will be forgotten in 500 years, but the global warming and associated sea level rise that we have caused will be passed on. Something that we change for 500 years or more, we change practically forever on the human timescale, and that is what we do to the climate – we change it forever.

[2] CE is an abbreviation for "common era" which is often used instead of "AD" in order to avoid the religious connotation.

Why does emitted CO_2 remain effective for so terribly long? The reason for this slow extraction from the atmosphere lies in the processes of the Earth's carbon cycle. This is being researched by thousands of scientists worldwide and contains a wealth of physical, chemical and biological processes and wonderful details. In essence, however, the socially relevant part is relatively simple. Of three carbon atoms with the chemical symbol C, which we oxidize by burning them with oxygen (symbol O) and thus turn into CO_2, one is dissolved in the ocean and thus becomes carbonic acid.[3] The other two remain in the atmosphere and increase the temperature of our planet via the greenhouse effect.

Once the extra carbon dioxide is in the atmosphere, there are few mechanisms to get it out again. Although there are strong carbon fluxes between the atmosphere and the land and ocean, these are essentially in equilibrium. The additional carbon we dig up in the form of coal, oil or natural gas is only very poorly absorbed by this cycle.

There are a few interesting permanent sinks for additional carbon. They lie in the weathering of rocks, the formation of humus and the sinking of organic material such as algae into the deep ocean. However, these processes are limited and very slow. Smaller temporary effects play a certain role; for example, it appears that in a warmer, more humid atmosphere with more CO_2 plant growth also increases at least in some areas, and plants naturally store CO_2 in leaves and stems as they grow. But these processes cannot permanently absorb the enormous amount of carbon we emit.

Unfortunately, this also means that becoming vegan does not really solve the problem, but only mitigates it. Agriculture and especially animal husbandry cause greenhouse gas emissions, which are very important for the current climate problem, but there is a fundamental difference to burning fossil carbon: The climate effect of agriculture[4]

---

[3] The resulting ocean acidification is an important and major problem. It attacks the ecosystem of the oceans. I won't go into it here, but it is obviously another important reason for stopping carbon dioxide emissions.

[4] And by this I mean, the contribution that does not come from burning fossil carbon, for example gasoline, or from cutting down trees.

disappears within a few years after we make it emission-free, while that of burning coal lasts for many centuries. The agricultural climate effect mainly results from fertilization and the associated emission of nitrogen oxides and the clearing of trees together with soil degradation. Contrary to what many people think, it does not mainly come from methane emissions from cows.

I would like to briefly clear up this common and fundamental misunderstanding: The electromagnetic rays of the sun and the Earth are of course indifferent to how a carbon dioxide molecule was created. Light does not care whether it interacts with a "fossil" CO_2 molecule[5] or a "modern" one. However, there is a fundamental difference between the carbon produced by burning fossil fuels and, for example, the carbon that we and other animals exhale or otherwise emit. The carbon emitted in the form of CO_2 or methane (CH_4) was recently ingested through our food. This food was either another animal or a plant. If it was another animal, then that animal either ate a plant beforehand or yet another animal. In either case, the carbon atom that we exhale was recently part of the vegetation. This vegetation has grown, taking carbon dioxide from the atmosphere and converting it into plant material through photosynthesis. The respiration of animals and humans and the photosynthesis of vegetation form a wonderfully complementary cycle. Oxygen and food are respired into carbon dioxide. Carbon dioxide and sunlight are synthesized into oxygen and plant growth. Just as the air that we breathe out is not causing the climate catastrophe, animal emissions are not the main problem of climate change. Methane emissions from animals contribute to the climate effect in a similar way to those produced by rice cultivation, because methane (CH_4) is a greenhouse gas about twenty times more potent than carbon dioxide (CO_2). In the atmosphere, however, it decomposes into carbon dioxide within a few years and is thus "neutralized" in the same way as the air that we exhale.

---

[5] That is to say, with a CO_2 molecule whose carbon was dug out of the ground in the form of oil, gas or coal.

There are many, many good and important reasons to eat less meat or no meat at all, and climate change is also a good reason.[6] But the methane problem from cattle is not at the centre of the climate problem because it is qualitatively different from fossil carbon. Climate change caused by cattle decreases immediately if there are fewer cattle on Earth. The climate change caused by fossil fuels will persist long after the fossil power plants have been shut down.

Figuratively speaking, plant growth, our food intake and the air we breathe out could be described as part of a *shallow* carbon cycle. The word *shallow* here describes the depth in time, if you like. The turnover rate of carbon here is weeks to years. In contrast, the burning of fossil carbon, i.e. coal, oil and natural gas, is an extremely *deep* carbon cycle. This is because these fossil deposits are tens to hundreds of millions of years old. To put it bluntly, they are the dinosaurs and their food, which have been compressed and converted over a long process of millions of years into the fuel that we pour into our power stations and combustion engines today.

During this time, carbon dioxide was extracted from the atmosphere and formed fossil fuels over many millions of years. Consequently, the warming we can expect if we burn all the deposits found in the Earth is comparable to the temperature of the Earth when the dinosaurs inhabited our planet 100 million years ago. I am intentionally drawing a simple picture here because this book is not about paleoclimatology. However, it is important to understand that the different areas of climate research, with their different methods and approaches, naturally come to the same conclusions. The fact that the entire planet was ice-free 100 million years ago, during the Cretaceous and Jurassic periods, is consistent with the findings of crocodile fossils near the poles and also consistent with the laws of physics and the computer simulations that are based on these laws of nature.

---

[6] In particular, reducing meat consumption is absolutely necessary if the 1.5 degree warming limit is to be met, which is the declared goal of all parties in the German Bundestag except the AfD.

These climate simulations show a global warming of around 15 degrees Celsius above pre-industrial levels if we burn all the fossil fuel reserves found. The physical calculations of the dynamics and thermodynamics of Antarctic ice show that this warming would make the continent ice-free (Garbe *et al.*, 2020). As Antarctica at the South Pole is home to the coldest mass of ice on our planet, this means that all other ice on Earth would also have melted and sea levels worldwide would be more than 70 metres higher. The results of climate research are based on the fundamental laws of physics, and over the decades they have painted an ever clearer and richer picture.

A variety of methodologies and disciplines illuminate the climate system from all sides. And it all fits together: Carbon dioxide raises the temperature of our planet, and it stays in the atmosphere for a very long time once it has been emitted. This means that the Earth's temperature will continue to rise for as long as we continue to burn fossil carbon. Conversely, this means that we can only stabilize our climate, i.e. keep it at a constant temperature level, if we reduce emissions to practically zero.[7] Then the CO_2 content of the atmosphere will no longer rise, and the temperature will no longer rise, or only for a limited period of time. It will then only fall again very slowly, but stopping the rise is the best we can achieve.

This is often described as "net zero emissions." The "net" means "below the line." In other words, we are effectively allowed to emit almost nothing – and we have to remove what we are still emitting from the atmosphere. Technologies that remove carbon dioxide from the atmosphere do exist. However, they are very energy-intensive and are not yet available on a large-enough scale. There is a lot to say about this topic, and a lot has been written about it. For the purposes of this

[7] Of course, climate is never stable in the sense that the temperature will be the same every year and everywhere on the planet. Some people can be very pedantic about this question, but this is nothing more than splitting hairs. What is meant here is that only if we stop burning fossil fuels can we achieve the relative stability that our climate had during the past 10,000 years of the era called the Holocene – the period in which we built all of our modern civilizations.

book, this discussion is not decisive, because in practice it does not change the factual zero limit for emissions.

Figuratively speaking, the atmosphere is a bucket that we fill with carbon dioxide. It is not a sink into which we can constantly pour something because it flows away again through the drain. That is a crucial difference. Because any warming limit we set, for example, of 1.5 degrees, 2 degrees or even 3 or 4 degrees is linked to a certain amount of carbon dioxide for precisely this reason – the atmosphere is a bucket, not a sink. This so-called carbon dioxide budget determines how much we can still emit if we do not want to exceed a certain warming limit. Compliance with this limit leads to folding.

At this point, I would like to make a brief excursion into two aspects of the carbon cycle that are relevant and not clear to many, but should not detract from the main message of this section.

These points concern two greenhouse gas sources that have a special role in the climate discussion. As mentioned, the carbon that animals and humans exhale was taken out of the air as carbon dioxide by plants for their leaves and stems and trunks a few weeks or years ago. In contrast, the carbon in coal, just like in oil and natural gas, has not been in the atmosphere for tens or hundreds of millions of years. It is true that this carbon was once also taken out of the air by plants, but in a completely different age, and afterwards this carbon was safely stored in the highly compacted fossil resources under the Earth.

In between the carbon of exhalation and that of fossil fuels, there is something else. And that is the trees. They are often centuries old and therefore represent very long-term carbon sinks. When we log down trees to create agricultural land or buildings, and especially when we do this in primeval forests, we add carbon to the atmosphere that had been out for a long time. In this case we are also warming the planet in the long term, just like when we burn fossil fuels.

Another extraordinary source of carbon is permafrost, i.e. the permanently frozen ground, especially in Siberia and Canada. When this thaws, biological activity awakens underground, which produces greenhouse gases. If oxygen is available, carbon dioxide, CO_2, is produced. However, if there is no oxygen because the processes take place in the muddy ground, methane, i.e. CH_4, is formed instead. In either case, greenhouse gases are produced that were not recently extracted from the atmosphere, but whose source materials were frozen for a long time. Just like burning or decaying trees, permafrost is therefore a source of additional warming when it thaws and then represents an important and, for us, dangerous response of the Earth system to man-made warming. It is an amplifying effect, but of course not the cause.

At the beginning and at the core of the climate problem is the burning of fossil fuels by humans. The resulting greenhouse gases change the energy balance of our planet and induce reinforcing feedbacks that increase the temperature of the Earth. Only if we stop emitting carbon dioxide can we stabilize our planet's climate. If we fail to do so, the destabilization of the climate, the accompanying fireworks of extreme weather events and the consequences for harvests and the economy will threaten to destabilize our society. This problem needs a solution. Things cannot go on as they are. It's as simple as that. But how do we do it?

6.2 Carbon Dioxide Needs a Limit and a Price

We need to stop burning fossil carbon entirely. To understand why this is so difficult, it helps to realize that the advancement of prosperity since the Industrial Revolution has been inextricably linked to fossil energy production. The associated technological progress is in turn closely linked to social achievements such as humane working conditions, the legal abolition of discrimination based on skin colour or sexual orientation and the emancipation of women. Even if it is easy for some people from their current position of prosperity to condemn economic growth because it is linked to destructive consumption, this is too simplistic for large parts of the world and also for large parts of our own history.

The development and spread of technological achievements have allowed us to satisfy our needs with greatly reduced labour, and this has enabled our overall social development. In relation to the poorer regions of the world, this puts us in a dilemma. Because, of course, people all over the world have the right to catch up towards greater prosperity where they lag behind the standard of living of highly developed countries. In today's economy, this means that the consumption of fossil fuels continues to increase in many poorer countries. However, it is precisely these energy sources, which until now have been seemingly inseparably linked to increasing prosperity, that we will have to say goodbye to worldwide within the next twenty to thirty years.

So how can we do this: expand global prosperity and at the same time move away from the use of fossil fuels?

There are various, but not infinitely many, ways to achieve this. The most obvious approach for many who are concerned about climate change is to simply ban carbon dioxide emissions. However, we must realize that our entire lives are so closely linked to this energy supply that a ban cannot happen overnight.

This is the first dilemma we need to resolve. Our CO_2 budget is extremely tight and our way of life is still extremely closely linked to the amount we still emit. Let me illustrate this briefly: The remaining carbon budget for staying within the 1.5 degree limit, which is considered necessary by many scientists and large parts of society to avoid dangerous climate change, is very small. If this budget were divided equally among the world's population,[8] the US would have used up its remaining budget within about five years (i.e. 2029) at its current level of consumption.

Let's try to get this scale really clear: A country in which around 70 million people voted for Donald Trump in the last presidential

[8] In other words, every citizen of the world would receive the same amount, i.e. be allowed to still emit the same amount until we stop completely.

election[9] in 2020 – people who, like their idol, deny climate change and consider any action against climate change to be a form of state terror – would have to stop burning carbon completely within five years. No more coal-fired power plants, no more gas-fired power plants, no more vehicles with internal combustion engines. People in Alaska would no longer be able to heat their homes with oil, people in New York would no longer be able to have their food delivered by gas-driven truck, people in Texas would have to turn off their air conditioning if not run by renewable energy. The USA would hardly be in a position to replace all fossil fuels with alternatives within the next five years. As a result, the power supply, the Internet and the food supply would collapse. I think it's fair to say that this would lead to a civil war in the USA.

And to make matters even worse, an equal distribution of the remaining budget among the world's population would not even be particularly fair. This is because Europe and the USA have caused the majority of emissions over the last hundred years. Accordingly, they should actually reach zero faster than the rest of the world. But that would shorten the deadline for the USA even further.

This illustration shows that an immediate ban cannot work. But it also shows that we have to accept that we cannot achieve a truly fair solution. Even if this is frustrating, it remains crucial that we solve the climate problem at all and as quickly and fairly as possible. Justice must be a central guiding principle here, and yet, sad as it is, it remains an unattainable ideal in a complex world. The practical solution is for all countries to go to zero as *quickly as possible*.

However, if an immediate phase-out of fossil fuels is not feasible, then a grace period must be built in and it must be announced that all consumption, extraction and import of these fuels will be banned, for

---

[9] The original version of this book was written before the 2024 election. Since then the situation has worsened significantly, but the illustrations here are still valid – in essence. The descriptions here are to illustrate the tightness of the carbon budget.

example, in Germany, in 2040. This would give industry and the population time to adapt to this new law. That could work.

A complete ban is also clearly feasible. It would be a limit in the folding sense: a ban in twenty years that gives us time to convert our economy, that would even help to generate innovation and jobs – therein lies the strength of a *folding limit*. In a way, this is the path that Europe is currently taking.

However, there is a further complication. A huge remaining question is whether such a limit will actually be enforced in practice if the implementation date is initially a long way off and then gets ever closer. A hard limit in the distant future requires a great willingness to act rationally, with foresight and long-term planning, not only in Germany but worldwide. It is questionable whether all sectors of the economy and private individuals will sensibly and slowly abandon the old technologies in the time remaining until the carbon ban comes into effect. This requires a strategic foresight that probably cannot be left to every individual and not even to companies in a sector as systemically relevant as energy supply. It is unlikely that all households will be able to manage without gas and oil heating in the year of implementation and that companies such as Exxon Mobil will have abandoned their current business model. We therefore need a way to guide this transition economically in order to ensure that it is implemented.

European carbon emissions trading is the political instrument for implementing precisely the kind of irrevocable limit that folding requires. The solution devised here is a combination of economic market dynamics and political limitation: *cap-and-trade emissions trading*. The "cap" stands for limiting the emission of greenhouse gases through emission certificates, the number of which is slowly but surely and transparently being reduced. The "trade" stands for the trading of these certificates.

Many people would perhaps prefer a pure incentive solution without a ban and would simply like to promote and subsidize renewable energies to such an extent that they drive coal, oil and gas out of the market. Unfortunately, this does not work. This type of economic mechanism has been studied for decades by economists such as Ottmar Edenhofer and his working groups and is also widely understood. The problem here is that, on the one hand, pure subsidization would lead to more renewables being used, but at the same time it would also reduce demand for fossil fuels, making them fatally cheaper and thus increasing demand. This simple mechanism – sometimes referred to as the rebound effect – means that less fossil fuels are consumed overall, but this reduction is greatly dampened. Since fossil fuels are effectively a gift from nature to the coal, gas and oil states, their price can be kept very low and it is almost impossible to get to zero carbon emissions in this way.

It is therefore not enough to promote renewables in order to achieve the socially desirable goal of zero emissions. This requires the setting of actual limits, if you don't just want to set a single phase-out date but to guide your economy by setting interim targets – then things get complicated. Zero means zero for everyone, but everything different from zero raises the question of distribution. Who is allowed to emit how much and when? Which economic sector has to phase out faster and which less quickly? Which company within a sector has to reduce, and how quickly?

If these questions are answered by the state, we will end up with a planned economy, and that brings with it a whole series of fundamental problems. A planned economy corresponds to hierarchically organized micromanagement and therefore has all the problems that such structures always have. Firstly, the solutions generated by a hierarchy can generally not be smarter and more innovative than the top that manages everything. This is a fundamental problem and has been documented in totalitarian regimes throughout history. The probability that a planned economy will find the optimal solutions is not very high. The question of which are the fastest paths out of dependence on fossil fuels in the various economic sectors can be better answered by companies than by a centrally governing political elite.

In addition, corruption in a planned economy is attractive for everyone involved; it makes the system sluggish and slow. We can't afford either when it comes to a problem as urgent as climate change.

One alternative is to put a price on carbon dioxide emissions and thus make the use of fossil fuels unattractive. The advantage is that the distribution of emissions among the various economic sectors can be regulated by the market, as can the distribution among the various companies. So you make renewables cheaper and fossil fuels more expensive until you get to zero.

There are currently two main methods of CO_2 pricing being discussed or applied. One is a carbon tax and the other is emissions trading.

The carbon tax is very simple to understand. For every tonne of carbon that is burned, a tax must be paid to the state – similar to the taxation of tobacco and alcohol. In this case, the price is usually not given for the carbon, but for the carbon dioxide. As the translation of one into the other is determined by physics,[10] it makes no difference. A carbon tax makes it economically less attractive to burn coal, oil and gas, thus creating an incentive to reduce the use of fossil fuels. The tax is easy for the population to understand and therefore transparent. On the one hand, this is a good thing, but it does pose the problem of acceptance. In order to increase acceptance and avoid burdening lower income groups in society, the revenue can be returned directly and in full to the population in the form of a so-called *climate dividend*.[11] If the climate dividend was the same for every inhabitant, then people with lower average emissions would make a profit and heavy emitters would be financially burdened. Since rich people's per-capita emissions are very much higher than those of less well-off parts of society, this social-buffering effect is significant. People with less than average carbon emissions would make net profit.

---

[10] A carbon atom has a molar mass of about 12 grams. Oxygen has about 16 grams. This means that one tonne of carbon becomes around 3.67 tons of carbon dioxide – 11/3 tons to be precise. The point being that the ratio is invariable.

[11] The idea of a climate dividend has been proposed by various people and institutions since the early 2000s. For example, by James Hansen in 2008. It was picked up by former US Secretary of State James Baker and proposed to US President Trump in his first term. In Germany it was proposed by the Mercator Research Institute on Global Commons and Climate Change (MCC), specifically by its director Ottmar Edenhofer and his secretary general Brigitte Knopf.

However, a fundamental characteristic of taxation is that it controls the price of carbon, but not directly the variable that is relevant for the climate – namely the quantity. In economic terms, this instrument achieves a clear reduction in emissions; however, those who can afford it will continue to emit CO_2. In order to control the quantity of emissions, it is therefore necessary to adjust the tax during the process towards zero emissions. You either have to drive them steadily higher or know from the outset at what price no economic sector will really emit any more carbon dioxide. Since companies will, of course, pass on the carbon tax to consumers, this will generate the impression among the population that the state's intention is to obtain money rather than to reduce carbon dioxide emissions. Although this suspicion can be countered by a climate dividend, it is likely to remain a constant matter of negotiation between politics, population and the economy. Keeping a carbon tax up and potentially increasing it, is thus probably not politically feasible over many legislative periods and different government compositions. A counter-example to this is Sweden, which has had a CO_2 tax since 1991. However, the Scandinavians are not yet at zero emissions either.

The alternative is emissions trading, which has been implemented in Europe since 2005. Here, emission rights in the form of certificates are distributed to various countries and various economic sectors therein. The number of certificates is regularly reduced according to a transparent long-term scheme. The price of the certificates rises as a result of the reduced supply. This method has the clear advantage that society controls the actual quantity of emissions. Companies can trade emission certificates with each other. As a consequence, the price of carbon emissions becomes the variable, while the total quantity emitted is controlled by the government: No more can be emitted than is permitted by the available certificates. This is a fundamental difference from the carbon tax, where it is the other way around.

Emissions trading in Europe had major problems in its implementation, especially in the beginning. In order to increase the acceptance of emissions trading more than 20 years ago, the allowances were initially distributed to companies free of charge. This made it possible for an enterprise to make a profit by selling surplus certificates that it did not need on the market.[12] In times when there was less awareness of the need for climate protection, this was a strong argument for its introduction. Climate protection was not expensive, but could bring in money. The incentive to reduce carbon dioxide was positive, not negative.

However, one immediately recognizes the problems that this creates. The fact that the certificates were given away meant that the EU had to decide which country would receive how many emissions, and the countries had to decide which sector and even which company would receive how many pollution rights. Market dynamics therefore applied to trading, but not to the annual distribution of allowances. Such a procedure is highly susceptible to corruption and inefficiency in finding an efficient and balanced distribution. As a consequence, the auctioning of certificates was implemented. The certificates are no longer issued free of charge, but are auctioned.

European emissions trading was a worldwide novelty when it was introduced and therefore had a number of "teething troubles," on which there is now extensive scientific literature. In the beginning, the CO_2 price was so low – and the number of certificates so high – that emissions trading was dealt with more in the marketing departments of companies than in actual strategic planning – it was used to adorn oneself as a "green" company, but no serious consideration was given to initiating the change in strategy necessary to reduce emissions to zero, i.e. to transition into a carbon-free economy. Professor Edenhofer and his group showed at the time that the emission price as traded on the market directly reflected what companies thought about EU policy in Brussels. It was a speculation on the steadfastness of the politicians rather than an actual market. During the financial and economic crisis of 2008 and 2009, fewer certificates were needed in the short term.

[12] However, the companies have actually made the most profit by attaching the carbon price to the end product (for example through higher electricity prices), even though the certificates were free.

The resulting increase in supply further reduced prices because the surplus certificates could be carried over from year to year, meaning that supply remained permanently higher than demand. For all these reasons, the price of carbon was, for a long time, so low that emissions trading continued to be used only for greenwashing and had no influence on companies' future planning.

Politicians did not dare to counteract the price dump and reduce the number of certificates, because the industry's argument was superficially sound: You have specified the amount that we should emit. If we emit less, then everything is fine, the target has been achieved. If, on the other hand, you reduce the certificates, then that shows that you don't actually want to stop climate change, but increase income for the states. No politician wanted to be told that, so the certificates remained on the market.

This argument is short-sighted, because the actual role of trade in this case is to help companies to perform the structural change towards zero emissions while being in competition within the market; only those who oppose change can see certificate trading as a punishment for carbon emissions. The German car industry is a good example of what happens if you resist for ideological reasons the necessary transition. VW and the other German car manufacturers simply slept through the transition to e-mobility while Tesla and Chinese e-car manufacturers made the transition and are currently outstripping them. However, emissions trading can only have a steering effect if the CO_2 price is high enough.

Even today, a small proportion of emission allowances are still allocated freely. However, an ever-increasing proportion is auctioned off. This makes trading less attractive for companies because it incurs costs. It also means that countries lose influence and are less able to pursue individual national interests. Auctioning is crucial to ensure that the market dynamics take effect as soon as the emission rights are issued. The price of carbon dioxide has now risen to a level that makes it a strategy-changing part of companies' calculations. Just as it was originally intended. In 2023, the price rose for the first time to more than 100 euros per tonne of CO_2 – something that seemed unthinkable just a few years earlier. This means that emissions trading is finally taking effect.

The decisive factor is that, in the case of emissions certificate trading, the state controls the quantity of emissions and not their price. This directly fulfils the politicians' mandate from the public, which is to stop climate change and not to make carbon dioxide emissions more expensive. The latter is only a means to an end. Even if the two factors are linked, the price of CO_2 and CO_2 emissions, it is still better, especially in the folding sense, to directly reduce or ban what we no longer want – as opposed to indirect regulation.

The actual task of emissions trading is to transfer the absolute limit of zero emissions, which will come in two to three decades, to the present. Certificate trading is intended to give companies an incentive to change their strategy today. In this way, it should make the limits set by the climate system tangible for the economy. Due to the time lag in the climate system, a lot of the consequences that we are causing now will not manifest for several decades. Emissions trading is intended to incorporate these consequences of our actions into economic dynamics, thereby inducing folding. The limits thus become part of the dynamics.

It is not about reducing emissions in the short term in a specific year, but about providing companies with a tool that makes it clear: The current production method will no longer work in the future, so companies need switch to a different, CO_2-free production method sooner rather than later. Emissions trading provides the time for this transition, but it increases the pressure from year to year so that the incentive for change becomes ever stronger. The sooner a company manages to switch to the technology of the future, the sooner it will be rewarded and have a competitive advantage over other companies.

If there is no incentive because the price is too low, then we have to hope that the boardrooms or even the shareholders will see reason. Emissions trading only fulfils its purpose if it supports this necessary rationality with a direct incentive. It took a while but is now working quite well. The certificate price has been between 50 and 100 euros per tonne of carbon dioxide since mid-2021 and must therefore be taken into account for companies' mid- and long-term strategies. The European Commission thus has an instrument to directly implement the emission reduction targets. For a long time, however, emissions trading at the European level was essentially limited to the energy and industrial sectors.

In December 2022, the EU Commission decided to introduce emissions trading for buildings and transport in its "Fit for 55" package, which is now called the ETS-2.[13] The interesting question here is whether two separate trading systems will remain in place. One argument against this is that the climate does not care which economic sector the carbon dioxide comes from. It makes no difference to the atmosphere whether the fossil carbon dioxide comes from a truck exhaust or a coal-fired power station. Economically, too, one could think that market power can best unfold if the same things – in this case CO_2 certificates – can be traded in one and the same market.

However, a strong argument in favour of separate systems is the fact that very different investments are required at the beginning to bring the various sectors onto a zero-emission path. These investments per tonne of carbon dioxide saved are significantly higher in the transport and building sectors than in the energy sector, and the CO_2 price should be higher here accordingly. If the trading systems were combined, the building and transport sectors would initially be able to afford the relatively low price without having to introduce transition strategies themselves. However, as the goal is the transition to zero emissions and trading is only a means to an end by rewarding structural change, separate markets are needed. This separation currently exists, but unfortunately the price distribution is the wrong way around. Politicians are worried that a higher price for transport would have a direct impact on consumers, which is why it is currently even lower than for electricity and heating. This must change quickly.

[13] ETS-2 = Emission Trading Scheme 2.

To summarize, I believe the following thoughts are helpful when assessing emissions trading. Firstly, the physically decisive factor is how much more we emit until we reach zero. It does not matter which economic sector the carbon dioxide comes from, and it does not matter when it is emitted. Emissions trading is primarily an aid for the economy to accompany the transition to zero emissions. It is therefore crucial that it generates a competitive advantage when a company embarks on a zero emissions path.

The folding as a narrative is very powerful because the absolute limit that is set is simple and transparent. This increases acceptance by the population. Such folding limits can be introduced for harmful substances such as carbon dioxide without the need to postulate the end of economic freedom. At the same time, the example of different carbon dioxide markets for the transport and energy sectors shows that more detailed instruments can be used and might be needed in order to facilitate the transformation towards keeping the limit. The simple rule of no more carbon emissions has another advantage, as I will try to show in Section 6.3.

6.3 Folding Instead of Forgoing

For a long time, the idea of environmental protection was associated with doing without. Given the enormous destruction that humans are causing on our planet, the idea that we need to consume less is a reasonable, actually an obvious one. However, the path that has often been proposed to achieve these goals is that of individual austerity.

It is very important to me to make it clear that individual renunciation of things that you consider wrong and harmful is a wonderful thing. It means that you are so strongly committed to something that you are prepared to make sacrifices. Since this ability to reason is something that distinguishes us as human beings, it is noble to act on it. I believe that many changes in our society arise from this willingness of individuals to make sacrifices. It is simply great to see people doing that. That people give up means of transportation that they consider harmful. Adapt their diet to their convictions and overall shopping in a way that is in line with their ethical beliefs. These individual actions not only have the direct benefit they are intended to achieve. They also have a radiance that can influence and convince others.

What does this have to do with folding? Folding is the process of setting morally justified limits for society as a whole and letting people live freely within these limits. For business and industry, the austerity of individual consumers is not something they can wish for. The system is geared towards growth, and growth here means first and foremost increasing sales. To this end, huge sums of money are spent on advertising, and the growth inherent in the economy is the driving force behind the global expansion of trade. Telling an entrepreneur or industry representative that we need to do less is tantamount to telling them to please refrain from competing with competitors and trying to survive. Any form of degrowth would be much more complicated than individual austerity and would only be possible if it involved a fundamental transformation towards a planned economy – the advantage of which I consider questionable for the many reasons already mentioned above.

If we accept for the moment that we have to solve the climate problem within the framework of the existing capitalist system, for no other reason than that it is urgent, then it is not very helpful to call on industry representatives to do less and wonder why this is met with rejection. However, if I tell the audience, as I have been doing for much more than a decade in my briefings to industry, that we have to accelerate reducing emissions as quickly as possible and innovate to bring them to zero in the foreseeable future, then that is something fundamentally different. The first reaction is always the feeling that "zero" is an extreme form of "less." But that changes immediately when people realize that to reach zero we do not have to do less, but simply something fundamentally different. Doing something differently is a concept the economy can work with, because "different" means innovation, means progress, not regression.

This is precisely the mechanism of folding. Based on the social understanding of a specific necessity, some large-scale limit is set that must not be exceeded. At the same time, society and the economy are given the opportunity to evolve freely within this boundary. A large number of players then start to look for new ways, and so they become creative and innovative. And that is exactly what we need to tackle our future problems – not just climate change.

6.4 The Solution to the Sustainability Problem

Avoiding the climate crisis is the declared future goal of many young people. What have we older people done if the young generation's utopia is merely the prevention of a creeping catastrophe? A utopia whose core consists of the mere hope of survival. This does not have to be the world we leave to our children.

In fact, overcoming fossil fuels can be much more than simply ensuring the survival of our democracy and our constitutional state. It can lead us to an almost fantastic future. If we get it right, solving the climate problem means not only avoiding the terrible risks of extreme weather and rising sea levels, but also that we as a human race can actually live eventually in harmony with our planet without sacrificing our civilizational achievements and prosperity. To achieve this, we need to go further than just introducing a carbon price.

We have already established that we will have to base our entire energy production on renewable technologies in the future. We also know that this is possible. Numerous studies have shown it, and it has only recently been summarized again in the latest Intergovernmental Panel on Climate Change report (IPCC WG3, 2022).

A common argument against an energy system that is essentially based on wind and solar energy concerns the fluctuations in the weather. There is unpredictability in the wind blowing through the turbines as well as in the blockage of solar radiation reaching the solar modules by clouds. These challenges can be met in various ways.

First of all, it helps if the electricity grid covers a large area in order to integrate wind and solar power across national borders. In Europe, there will always be wind somewhere because of the ground-level version of the jet stream. Sometimes it blows high in the north of Scandinavia, and sometimes it reaches as far south as Spain. But it always blows as long as our Earth is rotating on its axis and the Earth's axis is tilted. That too is simply physics. Weather systems typically have the size of a medium-sized country like France or Germany. So when a low-pressure system creates clouds in one place, there is a high-pressure system nearby that pushes the clouds away and provides a clear sky for solar energy. In between, there are geostrophic winds blowing through turbines.

This means we need pragmatic energy solutions for regions the size of the European Union. The US is big enough for a national solution, but it could consider including Canada and Mexico in its grid. China is also big enough. If friendly neighbouring countries were to agree on energy pacts, that would take us a long way towards energy and climate stability, and it probably would not be bad for the stability of peaceful coexistence either.

The second component of a renewable and stable solution is energy storage. This can be traditional storage, for example in pumped hydroelectric power plants, or smart but energy-intensive solutions in which renewable electricity is first used to produce hydrogen and then methane or liquid hydrocarbons as fuel. The combination of these two components is already sufficient and enables us to establish sustainable energy production that is stable and climate-neutral.[14] We can thus avoid a climate catastrophe, and that is great.

But what if we could do even more?

If we generate enough wind and solar energy to ensure a stable power supply, it will often be the case that there is too much electricity in the grid. At these times – and only at these times, not always of

[14] Smart technology for flexible energy demand is an additional component that can be very helpful. It is not absolutely necessary, but it makes the solution much easier.

course – electricity will have a negative price. This already happens occasionally for very brief moments. It means that electricity costs less than nothing. It means that in these moments people will be paid to use electricity because electricity generators have to get rid of it to prevent an explosion.

We can store this excess energy and use it later – as described above – but converting the energy back and forth will involve some losses.

In addition, or even as an alternative, we can use it to recycle material. A lot of material.

Because even if we solve the climate problem, we will still have a massive resource problem. Many of our planet's resources and materials, such as copper, phosphates, and rare earths, but also sand and fossil water, are limited, which means that they will run out at some point. This is actually true for every material on Earth – some are rarer than others. And even for those that are not scarce, waste is already a major problem today. This means that our aim must be to build everything we produce from materials that are either grown or that we have already used before. We have to get to a point where we essentially no longer mine raw materials at all. We have to get to a genuine circular economy.

For a sustainable ecological way of life, I therefore propose a second folding boundary in addition to the zero-carbon emissions boundary: zero resource extraction. Not immediately, of course, but in the long term. At some point, we should be able to stop using new raw materials.

There are an infinite number of things to consider and an infinite number of solutions to be found on the way to this folding limit: technical, economic and political. In the technical arena, for example, plastic would have a special role because it can essentially not be recycled; it also poses particular environmental problems due to the difficulty of disposal (microplastics in the sea, soil, organisms, etc.). Furthermore, we would not only have to recycle raw materials that have already been used, often with high energy input, but also make greater use of regrown raw materials, which is already happening to some extent today.

A cyclical production method requires enormous amounts of energy, because according to the second law of thermodynamics, energy is required to bring something back to its original state, and in this case a great deal of energy. It is true in general and a fundamental physical insight: Without energy input, disorder, or entropy, increases in a system. The original state can only be restored with the help of energy. Or to put it another way: Without energy, there will only ever be downcycling, but no recycling. Solar radiation and tidal motion are the only external energy sources that are constantly supplied to our Earth. Solar energy drives both the winds and the ocean currents. Tidal energy is much less powerful, but can also be harvested.

If we have the surplus energy from the renewable system, we can use it for recycling. If this is done in automated recycling factories, these factories could flexibly follow the electricity market. Recycling machines could run at times when too much energy is generated from wind and solar. This would benefit from a low or even short-term negative electricity price and would stabilize both the physical electricity grid and the economic electricity price.

Economically, the zero-resource folding limit would enhance the importance of repairing as well as recycling raw materials. Let us return to my somewhat artificial idea from Chapter 5 and assume that in the future particular prestige could be attached to driving a car for as long as possible. Companies like VW could produce significantly fewer new cars and convert a large part of their factories into repair workshops so that cars are driven for 25, 30 or even 50 years instead of two, five or ten. This would greatly reduce the need for new resources, and at the same time the jobs that are cut on the one hand would be needed on the other for services such as repair, maintenance and perhaps technical upgrades. This is just a small, perhaps seemingly naïve example; the economic transformation could continue to develop in the direction of more services towards the zero-resource extraction limit. The important thing is: This does not mean zero economic growth. In fact we would need the innovative power of the economy to fulfil the zero-extraction folding limit.

In addition, the sustainability limit of zero resource extraction would change a lot politically. Europe would not only become independent from the fossil fuels of Russia and Saudi Arabia, but also from the raw materials of China. Rare earths, for example, which are mainly found in the People's Republic, would be recycled instead of mined and imported. Today, raw material deposits are a decisive factor in the struggle for global influence and regional dominance. This logic would change completely if we stopped extracting resources from the Earth. The global economic network would be transformed according to new criteria. This does not mean that we resolve all conflicts on Earth of course, but some.

With the two ecological folding boundaries of zero emissions and zero resource depletion, we would create an incentive structure that not only solves the climate crisis, but allows us to really get to grips with the sustainability crisis as a whole. In the end, we may be able to stop exploiting our planet and only use what we have already drawn into our system, plus regrown materials.

The phase-out of different raw materials could follow the same path as that of carbon. We could introduce the equivalent of a carbon trading scheme with ever decreasing certificates. These certificates would not be for carbon, but for, e.g. plastic. One by one we would eliminate the exploitation of one raw material after another.

The sustainability limit of zero resource depletion is currently still in the realm of utopia. We do not yet know how to achieve it. But that does not mean it cannot be done. Many innovations have come a long way from the realm of fantasy before they became part of our everyday lives – from Leonardo da Vinci's dreams of flying to the fairy-tale journey to the moon. The two ecological folding boundaries describe a clear vision for the future; a vision of how the world could be made significantly better by using renewable energy and no longer mining anything. Humanity could live in harmony with its home planet, and we could offer our young generation a new utopia: a utopia of abundance instead of sacrifice. What a wonderful world that could be.

7 Folding the Economy: Competition and Diversification

> Life is complicated, Europe too… 750 representatives
> for 750 versions of what people actually want…
> Welcome to democracy, b**ch!
> *Christiane Paul as Ingeborg Becker in "Parlement" (2020)*

In the next two chapters, I will apply the concept of folding to two economic aspects of society and make suggestions as to how folding limits could be negotiated within society. It is important to make it clear that folding has its justification independently of these two applications that I am proposing here. You do not have to agree with these ideas in order to accept folding as a viable and feasible narrative. They are options that society could agree on, but they are in no way compelling. Independently, folding is an excellent narrative, and its concrete manifestation depends on the limits that are set. Society must decide on the concrete shape of these boundaries or *folding limits*.

When I propose three additional folding limits below – one in this chapter and two in the next – there is one criterion to bear in mind, despite all the political differences and perspectives from which one accepts or perhaps rejects them: the need to set folding limits at all arises from the fact that developments within our national and international societies have become dangerous. Dangerous for the system because they are self-amplifying. In their concrete form, the three limits I am presenting here are proposals that can be discussed and negotiated. There is no doubt in my mind, however, *that* we need such limits in view of the self-amplifying explosion that is built into our economic and societal systems.

7.1 Too Big to Fail

On good days, I see the economy as the engine of society because it provides the energy we need for our lives. But on bad days, when I think of developments in Russia or China, or the high levels of poverty in the USA, the economy seems more like a rabid beast. Either way, it is one of the central forces in our society, and it is not decoupled from us, but part of our life. It is shaped by us, and we use the products and services that emerge from it. Because it is the fundamental driving force for truly targeted and effective work to be carried out. I am also convinced that the speed at which the climate problem is solved will be determined by the economy. Politics, with its democratic legitimacy, must irrevocably prescribe the direction – namely global climate neutrality by the middle of the century. And politicians must set the appropriate framework so that it is economically advantageous to develop and use climate-neutral technologies. But the power and speed of the transition will then be determined by the economy.

In the spirit of folding, the instrument of choice would be a clear phase-out date for the burning of fossil fuels, a date for the zero-emissions limit. This would make this target part of companies' competitive strategy. If we succeed in steering the economy into a competition for the most environmentally friendly products – not for image reasons, but because it would be a decisive competitive disadvantage to miss out on the transformation – then we will achieve this goal faster than any politician would dare to prescribe.

The economy is essential for our society. However, to ensure that it does not behave like a rampaging beast but serves us as a functioning engine, we have long since introduced rules. These rules were created not only to prevent the exploitation of people, but also to ensure that companies and consumers pay for the functioning of the system that makes successful business and trade, and ultimately our daily lives, possible in the first place. I am talking about taxes.

Anyone who has ever received money for self-employed work and only had to pay taxes afterwards can understand why it hurts some people to hand over hard-earned money to the state. It is easy to forget that we can only earn this money because essential framework conditions for our economic activity are created with the help of tax money. Of course, this realization is not new, but is actually so trivial that it should not have to be mentioned at all. However, as in other cases in this book, it seems important to me to bring this fact clearly to mind again when making some of my arguments.

To be able to sell a Windows or Apple operating system, you need not only a functioning economic system, but also a legal system that confirms and defends the legitimacy of its value. It requires a virtual network infrastructure with all the material necessities to maintain it. It requires an energy system that is protected by the rule of law. It requires an education system that makes the use of computers possible at an appropriately high level. In fact, every good, whether material or virtual, and every service can only be produced and traded because society functions around it.

This functioning is made possible by taxpayers' money. We use it to pay for state services, for the rule of law and security, for education and roads, and so on. Herein it is also not a problem if the services provided by the state go beyond mere necessities. Financing culture, science and social peace is also justified in a democracy if the majority decides to do so.

These thoughts are, as I said, self-evident, but they show that economic life at the level we enjoy cannot exist without the state. As obvious as this may seem to us in Europe, it seems less obvious to a large number of US Americans who believe they can lead the kind of life they are used to without governmental organization. Even in some FDP[1] election manifestos in Germany, tax is sometimes portrayed as a handout to the state. Of course, one can argue about the specific structure of taxes. But they are not a handout.

My point is: The economy needs a functioning society and therefore a state, just as society needs the economy. The state and the economy

---

[1] Freiheitlich Demokratische Partei = Free Democratic Party.

are not competitors, but play together, and this interaction requires a balance. The balance is not symmetrical. In a democracy, the state represents the majority of the population. The so-called primacy of politics therefore prevails – within the framework of the rule of law. Against the backdrop of totalitarian regimes and overpowering administrations that can develop an undemocratic life of their own, it is always important not to allow the state to become overpowering. For a long time, Western societies were focused on this danger of an overpowering state. The dystopian visions range from Franz Kafka's *The Trial to* George Orwell's *1984* or the film *Enemy of the State* with Will Smith and Gene Hackman – the abuse of state power is an ever-present danger against which we must be vigilant. Self-amplification processes usually play a central role here too.

Today, however, another danger appears to have become much more urgent: Companies undermine democracy when they become too big. This danger is not new, but well known. Companies are threatening politicians to cut jobs en masse or relocate abroad, thereby influencing or preventing legislation. This power of the economy over politics has reached completely new dimensions since a group of companies have taken their leave from the competition within the market through practically unlimited growth: Google, Amazon, Meta[2] & co. These companies have almost completely undermined the primacy of politics over business in many areas, and not just within the country in which they are based, but in large parts of the world – which renders attempts by state actors to limit their power extremely difficult.

This is partly due to their size. There is currently an enormous monetary and political incentive for companies to grow and merge with other companies. In contrast, there is no relevant monetary incentive to split up. If you discover such an asymmetry in a self-amplifying incentive system, it is worth taking a closer look. In which direction does the asymmetry push the system? An asymmetry in the incentive

2 The merger of Facebook, Instagram etc.

structure will always lead the system in the direction of the higher incentive, i.e. in the case of companies, to become bigger and bigger. If it is also a system that allows for self-amplification growth – as in the case of companies – then it becomes dangerous.

During the financial and economic crisis in 2008 and 2009, the expression "too big to fail" became popular. Some banks and companies had become so large that their bankruptcy would cause the entire US economy, and therefore the world's economic system, to collapse. In Germany, companies of this size are often referred to in a more positive and harmless-sounding way as "systemically relevant."

In the case of 2008, it was banks that were rescued at great expense in taxes because their collapse seemed to be the greatest evil for society. But, of course, other companies can also be *too big to fail*. The existence of such companies is frightening. That our entire economy could hang on a single company is a breathtaking thought in itself. But when you consider that "the economic system" is not something abstract, but is responsible for providing people with food, clothing and housing, then this is an unacceptable situation. Consequently, US President Obama announced at the time that no company could ever again be "too big to fail" or "systemically relevant" in the future. This has never been implemented.

In most countries, we have antitrust authorities whose job it is to intervene when the growth of companies and the market power that comes with it threatens to undermine competition. However, companies such as Google, Amazon and Meta are proving that this is not working well at the moment.

When considering this failure, I am of course not concerned with the abilities of the employees of the antitrust authorities. Even the structures within such authorities are not really relevant here. What does not work and needs to be questioned is the concept of case-by-case decisions on matters of monopolies. The president of the German Federal Cartel Office, Andreas Mundt, said in January 2022 that "after less than a year" of analysis, his authority had "found a paramount dominance of Google within the market." This is a "very important step," as it means, according to Mundt, that the cartel office can "now take up specific action towards protecting competition[3]." However, a multinational, fast-growing and powerful company like Google cannot be confronted with this kind of tortoise-pace dynamic (and one might almost say somewhat mockingly: It's nice that the antitrust authorities have already noticed this in 2021). But, of course, the problem does not lie within the agency. It lies in the fact that society's response to the emergence of monopolistic companies is not dynamic and inherent to the economic system, but is imposed from an outside authority that is too slow. It is up against a dynamic self-amplification growth process, and it cannot win this battle.

In addition to the national limitations of the antitrust authorities, it is therefore a fundamental mistake that they decide on a case-by-case basis. This means that the consequences of their decisions are not part of the system dynamics, but an instrument that is actually more suited to a planned economy than a market economy. As they have to examine each individual case and negotiate politically, the antitrust authorities cannot really prevent an ever-increasing concentration of economic power in a few mega-corporations, even if that is their mandate. What is happening is a gradual disempowerment of the state and thus of the population by companies that are more powerful than the states in which they operate.

The emergence of platform economies has led to the rise of tech giants based on – to name just a few elements – mass data collection and social networks. In turn, the problem of corporate power has, as I said, taken on a whole new quality: the influence of a handful of (not only, but predominantly) US-based companies now extends to large parts of the world, and many national governments have so far had little means of limiting them.

If we want to counter this power at all, then we need to become aware of the possibilities and, above all, the legitimacy of the state again. In a democratic society, the state represents the population. No company

---

3 https://www.tagesschau.de/wirtschaft/unternehmen/bundeskartellamt-google-datenverarbeitung-101.html.

has this legitimacy, no matter how much is bought from it. Google has no right to decide how we live. This decision-making power lies with us, and we must choose how we want to best organize our interests.

7.2 Limits as Part of the System

Companies have a strong economic interest in growing and merging with other companies. There are many reasons for this: greater independence from suppliers, more efficient communication and management structures between the different parts of the company and, above all, market power. In contrast, there are practically no incentives for downsizing companies or splitting them into several companies with different products. This is why company mergers are much more common than the division of large corporations into several small or medium-sized ones, unless a company sells certain shares for economic reasons.

Corporations can effectively grow into infinity. When it became apparent in the USA in the 19th century that companies were exploiting their growing market power without restraint, the Sherman Antitrust Act of 1890 was the first competition law to be created in response to such undesirable developments. This was the birth of the antitrust authorities. The motivation behind their establishment in more than 120 countries worldwide is first and foremost an inherently economic one. Individual companies should not form monopolies, nor should companies join together to form cartels and undermine market dynamics with, for example, price agreements. The idea here is to protect the market and thus the consumer from the superior power of a company or group of companies that exploit their monopoly position, for example by charging excessive prices. After all, the capitalist incentive system is based on competition; only if it works does it prevent disproportionate price increases and promote innovation. Or, to put it in terms of the ability to control self-amplification processes: A problem always arises when a company leaves competition, i.e. becomes so strong that no other company can curb its increase in power. In ecology, this is called a plague – like the plague of rabbits that Australia is still suffering from today. They have been spreading en masse for a good 150 years, causing enormous ecological and agricultural damage. The plague is attributed to the original 24 animals that an English settler had brought into the country by ship in 1859.

But back to the economy. The monopoly position of companies that are too large and too powerful not only harms the market. During the financial and economic crisis of 2008 and 2009, it became clear that the "systemic relevance" of financial companies such as Goldman Sachs, Lehman Brothers and AIG posed a threat to the entire global economy. This made it very clear that we had made our supply of essential goods such as food and energy dependent on the existence of individual companies. Irrespective of moral considerations, this is simply not a sensible risk strategy. As discussed above, we create more stable conditions when we rely on a rich entrepreneurial culture. This applies not only to ecosystems and the internet, but also to our supply of goods and services. We need a supply system that rests on the broad shoulders of a large number of companies to minimize the risk of collapse.[4]

The idea of limiting corporate growth is not new and can be underpinned by various arguments. The idea of placing this task in the hands of government agencies is understandable. First of all, it makes sense to counter the potentially exponential growth of companies with a higher-level decision-making authority that can break this growth down into smaller units, which can then grow in turn. This approach takes account of the fact that, for example, a tax that only ever transfers a certain proportion of a company's profits to the state does not lead to a limitation, but only to a slowdown in the exponential growth.[5]

---

[4] Stability through chaos, or in other words diversity, has already been illustrated in Chapter 5.2 using examples such as the Amazon rainforest and the Internet.

[5] For the pros: An exponentially growing capital stock of a person or a company can be described by $K(t) = K_0 e^{t/\tau}$. If a certain percentage of tax, say θ, is taken from this, it only slows down the exponential growth but does change that it still is exponential growth. The coefficient but the exponential growth remains unchanged. All that is changing is that the time scale, represented by the τ changes into $\tau/(1-\theta)$. For form of the equation stays unchanged only with a different τ.

Analysing the exact mechanisms by which Google and Amazon manage to evade the antitrust authorities would go too far here. What is crucial, however, is that the goal is not achieved. The individual case decisions allow companies to influence or circumvent the measures by legal or other means. A possible limitation of corporate power is therefore not part of the dynamic economic system, but the subject of an external legal and ultimately political negotiation process. If, for whatever reason, society decides that the size of corporations should be limited – as it has done with antitrust laws – then this limit itself should become a central part of the economic dynamic. This makes sense for many reasons. Not least so that companies can incorporate these limits into their business strategies. Because then folding emerges.

One way of setting limits is through corporate taxation. There is extensive economic literature on the taxation of companies and also on how this can be used to introduce a *de facto* upper limit for companies. The decisive factor for folding in general is that you actually limit the thing that you want to prevent: in this case, that a corporation becomes more powerful than the sovereign state in which it operates. Therefore, the taxation of a company may only become uneconomical for the company when its size and turnover or profits come close to the size of state budgets. The budget of the Federal Republic of Germany is in the region of 500 billion euros per year.

You could therefore consider whether companies in Germany should be taxed in such a way that it makes sense or is necessary to split them up if their annual turnover is, for example, around ten percent of the federal budget, which would be around 50 billion euros. A company with an annual turnover of 50 billion is still very large. But it leads to more competition if you prevent growth beyond this limit. Of course, the specific figure needs to be discussed, thought through and negotiated. Does it make sense to set this limit at ten percent, or would three or five percent of the German budget make more sense? I am concerned here with the principle of setting a limit in relation to the budget size of the state, which represents the sovereign, namely the population.

In order to be able to think through the effects of such a size limitation measure in more concrete terms, let us discuss a very simple possibility here. Let's assume that the corporate tax rate on profits would initially increase linearly with turnover and then slowly flatten out so that it (as scientists say: asymptotically) amounts to one hundred percent for infinitely high turnover.[6] At 100 percent taxation, nothing is left for the company, so the incentive for further growth disappears well before this limit. As already mentioned, there is a literature on this problem (e.g. Riedel and Simmler, 2021; Wentland, 2023; Zimmerman, 1983). The specific implementation is not crucial here; it should just be as simple as possible and therefore transparent for everyone. Relevant within this book is rather the idea of a tax that would run up to 100 percent depending on the size of the company and thus define a *de facto* (but to a certain extent flexible) upper limit for corporations.

The fact that this limit is induced by a tax prevents it from being a hard number. For some economic sectors, it will be worthwhile to pay a higher tax than for others. The tax can be calculated on turnover or profit. Of course, there is a huge difference. However, I am deliberately not making this distinction here in order to make it clear that the implementation must be discussed and worked out by experts. My aim here is simply to think through what would happen if we limited the size of corporations with a volume of several billion euros or dollars without restricting entrepreneurial freedom below this folding limit.

This corporate tax would apply to each independent company individually. The antitrust authority would then only be concerned with checking whether a company is independent or part of another company to which its turnover or profit must be attributed. The advantages of such a taxation system are obvious. If a company becomes

---

6 For the thought experiment, the mathematically trained reader can imagine that the profit after tax G is calculated from the profit before tax U as follows: $G = G_{max} \cdot \frac{U}{U_{50} + U}$. The tax rate $t = \frac{U - G}{U}$ can easily be calculated from this. Society would have to agree on how high the maximum profit, G_{max}, of a company may be and at what turnover the tax rate should be 50 percent, U_{50}. These are the two parameters of the tax. G_{max} is the parameter that should be based on the country's national budget. With U_{50} as a free parameter, that can be used to control the tax revenue required by the state.

too large, it is divided into smaller companies as a result of corporate dynamics, which are part of the economic system. It would come from within and would not be a decision that would require political and administrative intervention. Let us think this through.

7.3 Growth into Economic Diversity

What would be the response to such a tax? First of all, the tax rate for small companies would be relatively low, as it starts at zero and then rises slowly. For most companies, there would still be the traditional incentives to become larger. From a certain size of turnover, which is based on the size of the state budget, there would be a clear fiscal incentive to split up. This would result in a range of maximum company sizes that would be different for the various sectors. After the division of an enterprise into, for example, two companies, there could still be business relationships between them. One company could be a supplier of certain product parts to the other. However, these suppliers would be in competition with others offering similar products, and they could also supply other companies. The two smaller companies would diverge in the medium term. The market would be enriched, the variety of products on offer increased and competition intensified. The limit would thus change the trajectory of the economy of the individual companies, the direction in which they develop and increase diversity in the economy as a whole.

This is folding in the sense of chaos theory. Growth in diversity. Qualitatively instead of quantitatively. The decisive factor for folding is that the division of a company is not decided on a case-by-case basis by a cartel authority, but by the company and its shareholders themselves, i.e. as a mechanism of economic dynamics. The exact implementation raises many important questions of detail, but conceptually decisive is the introduction of a *de facto* upper limit. This would be set so high that it would not mean a tax increase for almost all companies, but in many cases even a tax saving. It is explicitly not about generating more taxes for the state, but about generating a new dynamic. Targeted at the mega-corporations that endanger competition and often also society by having too much power over politics.

In the case of companies where the limit plays a role, no cartel office would make a lengthy decision on the market situation, but instead, as profits increase, an incentive would be created to split up into smaller companies and thus increase competition. It would be up to the shareholders to decide which development is more profitable.

In the US, the government has repeatedly decided to split up companies in the past. The reason for these decisions has always been shifts in competition due to the formation of monopolies. Each time, the total value of the companies involved has increased, as has the competition within the corresponding sector. The last government decision of this kind concerned the telecommunications giant AT&T. It took ten years.

The organization of such company splits via the tax system is much better because the question of the size and timing of the split becomes a calculable element of the company strategy. The entrepreneurs themselves decide on the split. Mega-corporations would simply be uneconomical. The system folds and generates more diversity and competition.

7.4 The Path Towards a Diversity Economy

Introducing such a drastic change is of course a challenge, and experts should analyse and advise on how this has to be implemented in detail. One of the problems that arises here again is that of national borders. How do we deal with the dilemma of the national limitations of decisions that affect internationally operating companies? The threat of company migration and the accompanied loss of taxes is used very forcefully by CEOs and shareholders to enforce their demands. We see at the moment how national economies suffer and people turn to demagogic populists politically, but the effect of creating jobs in poorer countries can in principle lead to a fairer distribution of wealth worldwide. It needs to be a balanced process in order to keep the democratic states prosperous. In contrast to the constant migration of money "upwards" to people who already have great wealth, a flow "to the side," i.e. to poorer countries, is something we could welcome in general. Workers in richer countries are then in competition with those in poorer countries. That has to be allowed.

Problems arise when labour in other countries does not comply with the laws in ours. Our way of life is currently dependent on production methods that we would not allow in Europe. This problem is so big that most people to whom I talk privately react completely helplessly to this mechanism. In response to this overwhelming dilemma, people for whom moral considerations are important take refuge in personal responsibility. They desperately try to do those things right personally for which they cannot seem to find a society-wide solution. In the wake of this, ethical labels have been booming for years.

I am convinced that we, as a state, should take back the sovereignty of our actions. This is not a radical declaration of war against multinational enterprises, but simply the conviction that we cannot give up achievements that we consider to be crucial and have developed over decades or even centuries of social debate, fight and even civil wars and revolutions.

And in fact we do not need to take this lying down. On the one hand, corporations want to produce in other countries. But on the other hand, they also want to sell their products in the EU and US. We still have the strong lever to decide which products can be imported into our countries and the European Union and sold here.

In every discussion on global environmental issues, such as climate change, the question of national borders arises. The completely justified objection to strong political measures is that a law regulating the economy leads to large companies moving abroad and producing there. If we then buy these goods and services, we have lost all influence on the production methods and environmental and working conditions. Of course, this objection applies not only to ecological aspects, but also to other rules that we consider to be right and have established. Ultimately, the reference to the threat of production migration means that we can only pass laws that do not impair the locational advantage that our respective country can offer. As a result, we are increasingly losing the opportunity to decide on our way of life.

This has been the case for a long time, and we have become accustomed to it, but it is not acceptable. It leads to powerlessness and a level of disenchantment with democracy that is dangerous. We are deprived of the opportunity to shape our society. We can no longer make fundamental changes to society because corporations operate globally and the Internet works worldwide, but legislation only works nationally.

In my opinion, we need to bring the decision-making power over our society back to our democratic institutions, and these are either at the state level or lie with the European Union. One possible solution is a generalization of the supply chain law that came into force on 1 January 2023 in Germany. Similar laws have already existed in France, the Netherlands, Switzerland, Austria and the UK for some time. A corresponding law is currently being prepared in the European Union. All of these concrete implementations are not yet far-reaching enough, but they could be the start of restoring the supremacy of politics over the economy.

The aim must be that only products whose production complies with the laws, or at least the fundamental laws of the country,[7] can be imported into a country. In the current versions, the regulations of the supply chain laws are still mainly limited to working conditions. Expanding them to include all social and environmental standards is a long way off, and it is clear that this will have a major impact on companies that produce abroad. They must ensure that the rules are adhered to and remain competitive at the same time.

Let us dwell on this aspect for a moment. There are two reasons that make production in poorer countries cheaper. One is that wages are lower elsewhere because the cost of living is lower. To a certain extent, the relocation of production leads to a reduction in wealth inequality,

7 Or higher legislative entity, such as, for example, the EU.

which is good because it reduces poverty. However, production can also become cheaper because social and environmental standards are lower. As we consider these to be right in our country, we must not relax them when we produce abroad. Just as companies must ensure that these rules are adhered to "at home," they must also do so abroad if they want to sell in our country.

The so-called Supply Chain Act could mean a turnaround by obliging companies to ensure compliance with human rights and social and environmental laws along the entire supply chain – including where raw materials are extracted or, for example, where production goods are being manufactured cheaply. The law thus transfers responsibility to the company for the circumstances under which and the materials with which something is produced. This responsibility for the supply chain is currently still quite limited. But the principle could provide a solution.

Imagine if you could only buy products in Europe that you could be sure complied with EU laws. This means that the working conditions comply with European laws, as do the environmental conditions. If that were the case, then we would have regained sovereignty over these central aspects of our lives and would not have to worry about the conditions under which every iPhone was manufactured.

The power of companies to migrate to other countries is matched by the power of countries to control what they import. Through this control of its sales market, the EU has enormous opportunities that we must slowly begin to exploit. Even though more than half of the world population lives within a relatively small sphere in Asia,[8] no really big company can afford to lose the EU and the US as sales markets.

In a sense, the Supply Chain Act is a response to the fact that the global community has not yet succeeded in enforcing certain standards at a global level. On the contrary. When states such as Russia and China, but also Iran, Saudi Arabia, Syria and many others, signed the United Nations Charter in 1945, which largely follows Kant's proposal for

---

[8] Enclosing India, Pakistan, China and Indonesia.

international law, the majority of the world's states agreed on certain values that emerged in the course of the European Enlightenment. Today, we are far away from this global unity. It is not only difficult to imagine that the global community is currently in agreement on new folding limits. It is even questionable how many of the founding states of the UN and many other signatories could still be won over to this charter today.

Nevertheless, a relatively small political instrument such as the Supply Chain Act does not change the fact that we can only solve the major challenges we face in the long term if we do so at a global level. This applies first and foremost to environmental problems. Zero emissions can only be achieved if everyone joins in – if countries such as China, Russia, India and even smaller ones continue to burn fossil fuels, we can at best slow down climate change, but not stop it. Therefore, in the long term, the folding limits can and must be thought of and enforced as universal boundaries – as distant and absurd as this may seem in view of the political situation in the world in the summer of 2023, when I am writing this down.

Just as human rights are incorporated into the legislation of countries in different ways, the implementation of other folding limits can also differ in detail. The Supply Chain Act would therefore be a concrete implementation of a folding limit, which could read: "Only goods and services whose production complies with the (basic) laws of the country may be sold in a country."

8 Folding Society: Incentive and Cohesion

> Some people get everything. Some people get nothing. Why is that?
> *Al Pacino as Johnny in "Frankie and Johnny" (1991)*

8.1 Property Pyramid and Tower of Power

In Germany, we live in a social and liberal democracy. It is liberal because it grants the individual the greatest possible freedom and the state largely stays out of individual life decisions.[1] And it is social because the state simultaneously tries to balance out excessive poverty. This is not so much about equality, certainly not in terms of wealth, but about equality of opportunity. The promise is that everyone, from any point in society, should be able to improve their circumstances through performance. A certain degree of inequality is acceptable in democratically constituted states, partly because this performance- or merit principle,[2] which rewards effort and is reflected in social and monetary appreciation, is an important driver of social development. I am currently unaware of any system that can determine these values better than the negotiation between people – what we call the market.

However, it obviously becomes difficult when the inequality exceeds a "certain level." This idea is not new. Almost all democratically constituted states try to compensate for excessive injustice through

[1] The term "liberal" is disparaged by the political right in the US. It is used almost as a synonym for "socialist," which is almost opposite to its actual meaning that derives from "liberalis," meaning "free-born." I use it here in the proper way, which is the way it is used everywhere but among the US right.

[2] I use merit principle here for the German word Leistungsprinzip although it is not a direct translation as I understand. It describes the principle that performance rather than inheritance or privilege.

appropriate social systems (education system, healthcare system, social insurance). Until now, the focus here has mostly been on avoiding severe poverty. In the meantime, however, great wealth is increasingly causing us problems.

When I propose below to draw two further economic folding limits, it is first important to understand that it is not the market, i.e. the negotiation process, that causes the problems, but certain self-amplification processes within our market economy. As we have seen above, one of the characteristics of self-amplification processes is that the associated growth is quasi-linear up to a certain point, but then explodes (Figure 3). Where it explodes, this exponentially increasing growth destroys the market with its free competition, as I showed in Chapter 7. Since antitrust law is obviously only insufficiently capable of preserving competition – a problem that has reached a new level with the mega-corporations Google, Meta and Amazon – I propose taxation as a folding limit for companies that limits infinite growth to a healthy level. Some may not see taxation as the best way forward – what is important to me is *that* infinite growth of one company is limited. *How* that happens is part of the political negotiation process.

However, there are also self-amplification processes in the area of private wealth that harm and will ultimately destroy our society. Our financial system is constructed in such a way that anyone who has money can make more of it. They practically do not have to do anything.[3] Those who have a lot of money can do so on such a large scale that they do not have to work. Sooner or later, especially if these assets are inherited without restriction over several generations, this self-amplification increase in wealth explodes. The wealth gap then no longer increases linearly; instead, a class of very rich people emerges who separate themselves from society. Those who belong to this financial elite have opportunities that others do not have and, crucially, that they can no longer achieve by performance.

---

[3] Fun fact: In economics, money that you receive without having actually performed a service is called a rent.

The problem always arises when the growth of assets explodes. Here, too, it depends on the scale. In Germany, these are assets very often inherited over several generations: if their growth is not interrupted, their increase follows an exponential curve (Figure 3).

In the beginning, the differences grow moderately, but this changes as more is added on one side. Many people know the famous Indian legend of the grains of rice on the chessboard. According to this legend, Sissa ibn Dahir asked for rice as a reward for inventing the game of chess. The king was asked to place only one grain of rice on the first square of a chessboard and two on the next, doubling the number of grains from one square to the next. The result is exponential growth, just as if the difference between people were doubled in each generation. In the beginning, the whole thing still seems acceptable. One grain of rice becomes two and then four and then eight. But by the 54th square, there is a pile of rice as high as the Eiffel tower in Paris.[4] On the 64th, the last square of the board, there are 18 trillion grains of rice. That is an amount that would cover the entire Federal Republic of Germany with a one-metre-thick layer of rice. The assets of the richest people in the world are about as far removed from our assets as this one-metre layer of rice covering Germany is from a sack of rice. It is not a question of prohibiting people from having different amounts of money. One person may have one sack of rice while another has a hundred. The crucial issue to keep our society functioning is to prevent one person from having as many sacks as another has grains. To achieve this, growth must not increase exponentially over generations.

However, the exponential drifting apart of society due to an explosion in wealth does not only happen at the transition from one generation to the next. In contrast to Germany, in the US the speed at which the wealth of individuals is growing already creating differences within a generation that can no longer be grasped with intuition. Exponential market developments such as Amazon or Tesla are breathtaking.

[4] A little hint for connoisseurs: Piles of rice grains are in a self-organized critical state and have a universal shape. A pile of rice is therefore clearly defined by its height.

Please note that I am in no way concerned here with the question of whether these are fair or not. That might be surprising to most, but I do not think that we need to have a fairness debate.[5] Exponential wealth needs to be restricted simply to keep our society a society. That is a much lower goal than fairness, and it is one that everyone should be able to agree upon. Without a society, there is nothing – not even wealth. Amazon clearly provides a service for society that is used and wanted. The value of this service cannot be ignored. Tesla initiated a revolution in the automotive industry that was actively blocked by other car manufacturers for at least a decade, and initially built up the market for electric cars almost single-handedly. We need an incentive system that sparks and inspires such innovations.

At the same time, the growth in wealth of the Amazon and Tesla bosses is literally unimaginable. In 2020, Jeff Bezos' wealth increased by 75 billion US dollars in one year. That's more than 8.5 million per hour. You can twist and turn these figures however you like. You cannot really get an intuition for them. Elon Musk's fortune increased by 121 billion US dollars in 2021. That's 13.8 million per hour. I'm just picking out these very well-known people here to illustrate the problem. This means that these two men each earn far more in ten minutes than a nurse can earn in a lifetime.

Without being distracted for a second by envy and resentment, I would argue that the wealth gap between men like Musk and Bezos and ordinary service providers like a nurse is bad for society. The global spread of ideas and businesses at an unprecedented rate is allowing an unprecedented explosion of wealth that is destroying the community of human beings. But we need this community, because without it, nothing – not even entrepreneurship and prosperity – is possible.

The unequal distribution of income and wealth is often measured with the Gini index developed shortly after the Second World War. This has a value of zero in the case of completely equal distribution,

[5] Even though we could have a fairness debate, and people do.

and if one person owns everything, it has a value of one. In Germany, China and the USA, the income Gini index has risen more or less steadily over the last thirty years. In Germany, it is currently around 0.3 – which could in principle indicate that most incomes in our society are not that far apart. Globally, the value has fallen slightly, but is still at a frightening level of almost 0.7, i.e. closer to the actually absurd value of one.

Unfortunately, this Gini index is no longer a good measure of the inequality we are experiencing. In a sense, it describes a *mean* inequality that does not adequately capture our problem. This can be illustrated with an example. The Gini index value for income in Germany of around 0.3 can result from very different situations. For example, it could describe a society in which each income occurs exactly once, i.e. if exactly one person earns 10,000 euros a year, exactly one other 10,001 euros and yet another 10,002 euros. With 45 million people in employment, exactly one person would receive these 45 million euros.

This is a constructed example for illustration purposes, in which the lower-income half receives on average exactly half as much as the higher-income half. This obviously does not correspond to an equal distribution, but rather to a kind of income pyramid. Whether it could possibly be a reasonable distribution for a fair society is open to debate – I doubt it is perfect, but it is not too bad either.

The crucial point is that the same value for the Gini index is also obtained with a completely different distribution of income, namely with a kind of income tower: if everyone earned the same, say 10,000 euros, but 45 people received five billion a year, i.e. 500,000 times more. In this case the Gini value would also be 0.3. These two societies are very different, although a pyramid of wealth and a tower of power above a flat level of low incomes have the same Gini index (Figure 5). Currently, wealth is increasingly concentrated among individuals. This means that as the rich in particular are becoming richer and richer because their wealth is exploding, the distribution in our society is

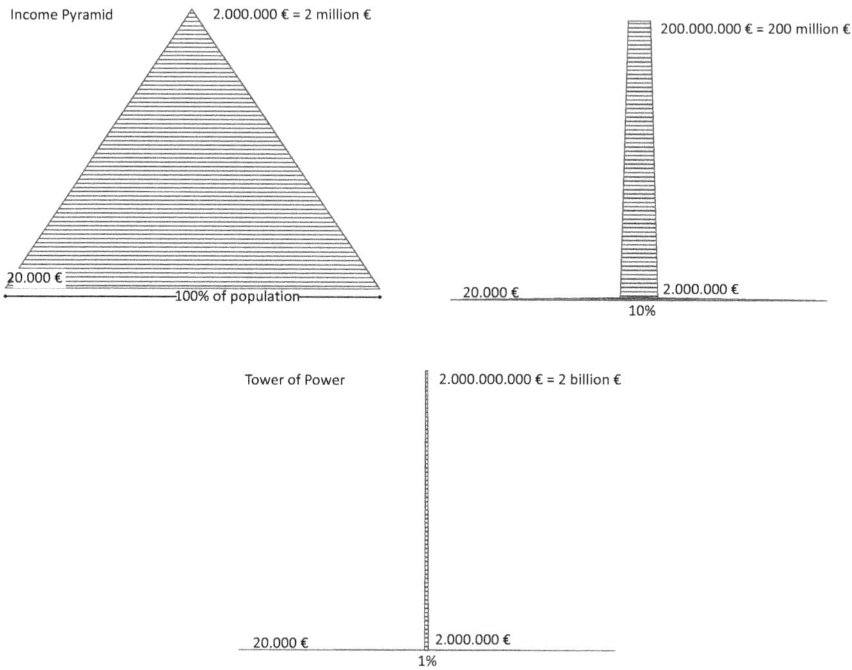

Figure 5. Illustrative income distributions in an imaginary society. This is a visualization of the scales and the concept. In the pyramid (left), income is evenly distributed among the various income groups. On the right, the same (!) pyramid is joined by a group of ten percent of the population who earn a hundred times more than the richest in the pyramid. From the perspective of these people alone, it is practically the same whether someone earns twenty thousand or two million euros a year, i.e. for them the pyramid is no longer visible. In the tower of power (bottom), the group of the richest earns two billion a year and has shrunk to one per cent of the population. The Gini index for the pyramid is 0.3, just as it has been for years in Germany. However, it is the same value in a situation in which basically all 45 million people in employment in Germany earned the same twenty thousand euros per year, while 45 individuals received ten billion per year. This distribution would be even more extreme than the one illustrated in the chart below.

developing in such a way that it corresponds to a tower of power. This fact is lost in the Gini index.

This is why actors such as the international aid organization Oxfam try to describe the enormous inequality with other measures.

Their report from January 2026 states that the richest 12 people in the world have more wealth than the entire poorest half of the world population. In other words, more than four billion people combined.

8.2 Self-Amplification of Real Estate Assets

Exploding assets in the real estate sector play a special role. Real estate differs from many other economic sectors in that it has an impact on economic and private life as a whole. If I buy an Asian meal from a street vendor in New York City, for example, I pay about ten US dollars for it. If I order the same dish in a restaurant right next door and sit down at a table to eat it, it will cost me over 50 dollars. It is probably of a slightly better quality and is brought to my table. But the difference in price does not primarily go towards the waitress's salary or the ingredients of the food, but largely towards the rent paid by the restaurant owner to the owner of the real estate. The majority of my 50 dollars thus goes to the owner of the property. Through this mechanism, real estate prices raise the cost of living in a city by increasing rents. Rents not only increase the restaurant bill, but also what a waiter has to earn to live reasonably close[6] to his workplace. Prices in Manhattan supermarkets and all other stores are rising along with rents, and with them the overall cost of living. Through real estate prices, a sharp stream of money flows directly upwards to the people who own the real estate, while those who are affected by the rising cost of living do not earn anything from it. Again, this is not about demonizing property ownership *per se*. The sector naturally performs a social service. Houses are built and renovated to create more living space. The problem arises when profits grow exponentially after the acquisition or repair costs have been paid off. This is aggravated by the so-called concavity of the utility function: The wealthier you are,

[6] And by that I don't mean in Manhattan, but somewhere within a radius that allows him or her to get to work within two hours.

the more money you need to achieve a perceived gain in prosperity.[7] This creates an incentive to demand an ever higher profit margin the more you already have. This reinforces the self-amplification dynamic not only in the real estate market.

8.3 Exploding Assets Jeopardize Society

In constitutional democracies, we have rules that formally guarantee that people have the same rights in court and that everyone's vote counts equally in elections. In practice, this does not lead to real equality before the law, even with relatively moderate differences in income, because not everyone has the same opportunities to understand the legal situation or to hire someone to do it for them.

In the United States of America, this also applies to political influence. The decisive factor for the outcome of elections is which candidate raises the most money. This is openly communicated by political commentators and party strategists. The reason is that money can be directly translated into votes – similar to how advertising increases a company's sales figures. Regardless of how well we understand these connections: Advertising leads to sales, and the funds of a political party lead to votes. This is why the opportunities to support parties with financial donations are very limited in Germany and are subject to strict rules. This is fundamentally different in the USA. There would never be a donation scandal like the CDU under former chancellor Helmut Kohl had. And one can certainly ask how democratic the elections in the world's oldest democracy really are, not only, but also because money has such a strong influence on the outcome – a predicament that is accepted by many in the USA.

The situation in the USA is just one example of how problematic it is for the cohesion of society when people with a lot of money leave

[7] This assumption has been established in macroeconomics for more than a hundred years. It is quite obvious and generates a number of social problems.

the framework of social rules, i.e. when they have power before the law and in politics that they are not entitled to according to the rules of the democratic idea. Examples of this systemic problem include the financing of the Republican election campaign by oil magnates Charles and David Koch and the rise of Donald Trump, which was planned over decades and would probably not have taken place without the Fox News channel, financed by Australian media mogul Rupert Murdoch with the declared aim of exerting political influence. But the role of billionaire Michael Bloomberg in the Democrats' election campaign against Trump should also be mentioned here, and Alexander Soros, son of "philanthropist billionaire" George Soros, has just declared that he will use his father's inherited fortune to become even more politically involved.[8] These opportunities to make politics with money do not arise from a mere difference between the wealthy and the less wealthy, but solely in a financial elite.

The explosion in the wealth of a few rich people poses a threat to democratic societies not only in the US. Their influence may be less obvious here in Europe – but it is still enormous. The problems that arise from this are manifold. On the one hand, money that is generated on the financial markets without performance – precisely because it is not earned but gained through speculation – is withdrawn from the system elsewhere. For example, stock market traders bet on the bankruptcy of countries, and taxpayers' money flows into bank bailouts and is then no longer available for the social systems. When Greece had to be "rescued," profits on the stock markets rose, while the harsh austerity measures drove many people in Greece to financial ruin and not a few even to suicide.

On the other hand, the super-rich have also been influencing the political system in Europe for years; for example, the media empire of the late Italian ex-prime minister Silvio Berlusconi contributed

8 https://www.spiegel.de/politik/deutschland/news-des-tages-donald-trump-alexander-soros-ampelkoalition-heizungsgesetz-arbeitsstress-a-4581ba18-5990-4a8a-81ae-8fadd4afff87.

significantly to the rise of the right-wing populists in Italy. The damage may be less immediate, but it is no less consequential. This includes the fact that if we allow very few to accumulate astronomical sums, we destroy the incentive system. People who are born with wealth that allows them to live without contributing to society have left the incentive system. They may continue to do business, invest and run companies, but they do so in a sphere of wealth detached from the normal population and normal companies – with almost unlimited scope for action and influence. In addition, there is the much-discussed loss of incentive for population groups who see no possibility of entering the middle of society anymore, let alone achieving real prosperity. If these two groups grow, our society is in danger of being torn apart.

There are good reasons for limiting – not eliminating – the difference between rich and poor in society. The decisive argument for me personally is that we as a society need a certain degree of cohesion, on which we all depend. What it means when this cohesion is lacking can be seen in many autocracies around the world. It is no coincidence that dictators from Saudi Arabia to North Korea put themselves in the hands of Western doctors when they are ill and send their children to school in Switzerland or England. The countries they rule do not provide services of anywhere near the same quality. The prosperity of even the smallest, wealthiest political caste depends on the existence of Western democracies in which a broad, relatively prosperous population produces and supports well-functioning systems – an education system, a health and social system, a well-functioning judiciary and administration. The fact that these systems are also increasingly under threat in our country can be seen by looking at the nursing crisis or the shortage of teachers in schools and doctors in hospitals.

So when I propose two additional folding limits here with regard to the development of wealth, I am not doing so out of moral considerations of justice – even if such considerations are of course justified. I believe that the undesirable developments that we are currently observing threaten the very existence of our democratic and constitutional societies and the rule of law. We should all be able to agree that these properties need to be preserved.

8.4 Limiting Exploding Assets Through Inheritance

With regard to wealth growing exponentially through inheritance, the first limit could be to agree on a maximum amount of money that one person can bequeath to another. The exact amount would be a limit set by society – a limit that can exert force in the sense of folding. The limit should be chosen in such a way that it serves only one purpose, namely to equalize the starting conditions for people to a reasonable degree. Of course, the concrete inheritance limit should be the result of a social negotiation process. It could be based on what you can earn with your own efforts in a finite period of time. I will argue later that there should be a maximum ratio of upper to lower income in a society. One could take this upper annual income as a measure for the inheritance limit.

Since scales are crucial here, let us consider a value to illustrate what this limit might be about. Suppose society were to agree that one person cannot bequeath more than two million euros to another person. It is important to be clear about the value of two million, because the scale is actually decisive here – not as a precise number, but as a concrete one. It is not a question of considering whether it is right in principle to be able to bequeath money. It is about the scale. Most people do not have two million to bequeath at the end of their lives. But others do, and there are quite a few of them. Let us take a look at what happens if someone has more than two million to bequeath. First of all, it would be permissible to bequeath to more than one person. If you have two children, for example, you can bequeath four million of your assets. If you have nieces or nephews or grandchildren, the amount of the inheritance increases quickly. But it increases linearly. Next, you can consider whether to leave money to friends or to organizations. This concept is not about giving the money to the state. It is about ensuring that it does not remain with one or very few people who have done nothing for this wealth. The concentrated transfer of wealth is a crucial breaking point in our society. Folding wealth that has accumulated at the end of a lifetime back into society can prevent an exponential divergence of society.

It is important for me to emphasize that for more than 98 percent of the population in Germany, this limit would not change their inheritance intentions.[9] You could even completely eliminate inheritance tax below the threshold. For the majority of the remaining two percent, it would only change how the inheritance would be distributed. The crucial thing is to prevent the development that is already threatening the cohesion of our society today: the unlimited inheritance of huge fortunes, which is slowly turning the group of the wealthy into a class of the wealthy.[10]

8.5 The Proportionality of Income

The second limit concerns the accumulation of wealth through income. Let us assume that it makes sense and is necessary for the cohesion and even the existence of society to limit the maximum income. A few years ago, Switzerland voted on a law with a similar objective. It would have stipulated that the highest salary in a company could only be twelve times as high as the lowest. Under such a law, no one would earn more in one month than anyone else in the whole year. The law did not get a majority and was therefore not passed, and I think that

[9] In 2020, around two percent of inherited sums in Germany were over one million euros, i.e. less than two percent were over two million.

[10] I use the distinction between social strata and class here in the sense that a class structure cannot be broken through a person's normal work. Class membership is inherited and cannot be acquired. There may be exceptions to this, as the inventors of Amazon, Tesla and Facebook show, but in general class structures are cemented, while stratification of society is an acceptable process, at least to me, because it is part of an incentive structure.

was because the ratio was set too low. I think income differences should be allowed that are greater than a ratio of one to twelve. But not infinitely large.

Let us think through such a limitation in principle. Since I do not believe that wealth should be prevented so that it does not lose its function as an incentive for society – and because it is unfair if performance is not reflected in income – this is also about a scale. The thought experiment must therefore be carried out using concrete figures. However, I want to stress again that the actual limit of the permissible ratio between the highest and lowest incomes, should it ever become a political reality, must emerge from a social, democratic decision-making process.

For illustrative purposes, let us assume that the minimum annual net income in Germany should be around EUR 20,000. This is just over 1,600 euros per month and is chosen here only as the roundest possible annual sum, which is not too far removed from the reality in Germany in 2023. If we could now agree that no one should earn more in one year than another person earns in their entire life, then we could generously translate this to mean that the maximum income should be one hundred times the minimum income. That would mean that no one could earn more than two million euros a year – after taxes!

For anyone who fears communist conditions if the maximum income is capped, just try to imagine having an extra two million a year in your bank account. A state in which someone can earn a net income of two million a year while someone else earns 20,000 is not a communist state. In addition to the fact that the production goods are not socialized and there are no other conditions like those that prevailed in communist states, with state-controlled media, etc. Two million a year makes you rich. It means that you can accumulate almost 100 million in fifty years of working life. That is an enormous amount of wealth, but at the same time it is a far cry from what is currently happening with the described fortunes of some of the super-rich. It would prevent the explosion that we are seeing with the highest increases in wealth.

The idea of a maximum income is not new. There is extensive economic literature on this topic. In practical terms, there are various ways to implement such a folding limit. One possible way would be to allow the tax rate to rise until it asymptotically reaches 100 percent for infinitely high gross income. This would be possible with a simple mathematical formula.[11] But, as I said, there are also other ways.

A folding limit that slows down exponential growth at one end of the scale is perfectly in line with the performance principle and the need for an incentive principle. If we can agree on such a limit, then it may be possible to turn the tower of power that the distribution of wealth in our society is threatening to become, or has perhaps already become, into a pyramid of prosperity again (Figure 5). The crucial difference is that the tower towers above the rest of society; those who live in it are enthroned above it, detached, with a great deal of power and influence that is not politically desirable and often invisible. The pyramid, on the other hand, is a cohesive society in which equal opportunities and equal rights are possible.

People are not equal, and therefore their importance in society does not have to be equal either. The consequence of this insight is that material remuneration does not have to be equal either. However, every social position must be attainable through performance. The natural differences in the abilities of family members, for example, should allow for advancement and relegation without the principle of merit being abolished by inheritance.

---

11 For example, you could use the same formula as above for company tax. The net income N would be calculated from the gross income B as follows: $N = N_{max} \cdot \frac{B}{B_{50} + B}$. This formula has two parameters that society must agree on. The first is the maximum net income N_{max} just discussed. The second is the gross income at which the tax rate is 50 percent, B_{50}. This could, for example, be determined by how much tax revenue the state needs. It would result in a directly perceptible link between government expenditure and net income. Everyone could calculate their own tax immediately.

8.6 Another Limit, for Limit Lovers: Ultra-Fast Trading

Boundaries do not always have to relate to an amount, and they do not always have to be upper limits. But most importantly, it is crucial that we set very few folding limits and that we are aware of these boundaries. The point is to maintain freedom by protecting ourselves from developments and self-amplifying processes that threaten something important. Accordingly, every boundary must be well and clearly justified. Folding limits are not meant to describe the path, but avoid the danger zone.

I would like to outline another possible limit here and put it up for discussion. The value of companies on the world's stock markets is now largely determined by algorithms. The trading of shares today often happens so quickly that it is beyond human perception. Algorithms, computer programs, are written to maximize profits by observing and trading share prices. The programs make decisions in nanoseconds. This means that a billion transactions take place within one second. Of course, one major danger is that these algorithms contain self-amplification mechanisms and lead to explosive events on the market, either by themselves or in conjunction with other algorithms.

First of all, nanosecond trading naturally involves the same self-amplification processes as any stock exchange trading. For example, if someone sells a large proportion of shares in a company, other participants may think that this share is worth less and sell it too. Demand for the share would then fall, even though its price is falling. This would lead to a downward spiral that self-amplifies. Normally, in a market economy, demand increases when the price of a good falls, but here it is the other way around. Depending on the exact situation, such goods are sometimes referred to in economics as Giffen goods (Jensen and Miller, 2008) or Veblen goods (Bagwell and Bernheim, 1996; Veblen, 1899). These terms are used in slightly different contexts and also differ. However, the property I am referring to here is that demand decreases even though the price decreases. This generally means that the negotiation for the price of the good is not converging. The negotiation is not concluded. No equilibrium is reached. The price plummets. The reverse works in a similar way. A good whose demand increases, even though it becomes more expensive, leads to a price spiral, as we occasionally see with luxury goods. The more expensive the Gucci bag is, the more people want it.

This type of self-amplification is dangerous even without nanosecond trading and leads to stock market crashes occurring much more frequently than "natural" disasters. A number of studies have shown that the statistical distribution of share price fluctuations corresponds to a so-called one-over-*f* distribution (Bak, 1999). If *f* is the size of the price drop, then this occurs with a probability that corresponds to the reciprocal of the size. So an event of size 10 occurs with a probability of one-tenth, 0.1. An event of size 100 has a probability of one-hundredth, and so on. The stock market can therefore be regarded as a so-called self-organized critical system. In practice, this means that collapses occur more frequently than we are used to in nature. Snow avalanches and earthquakes follow a similar distribution. This has very practical consequences. One of them is that it is no longer possible to calculate an average damage value, as this would be infinitely large. As a result, there is no real insurance against this type of accident, because the average amount of damage determines the price of the insurance; thus, the insurance would have to be infinitely expensive.

This phenomenon, like the risk of the collapse of "systemically important" banks and companies, has the potential to severely damage the global economy or even cause it to collapse. In the case of natural disasters, such as earthquakes, which follow such a probability distribution, the state generally steps in and saves the insurance companies, so to speak. But a global stock market crash has a different dimension, and we, as a society, have to ask ourselves whether we want to bear this risk, one with a mathematically infinite volume of damage.

In stock trading, the trading frequency determines the Lyapunov exponent of the self-amplification process. If this frequency is in the nanosecond range, then it is the same time scale as an atomic bomb. The amount of damage doubles a billion times per second. That is very fast. In a sense, nanosecond trading has introduced an atomic bomb into the financial market. Humans can no longer intervene to stabilize such enormously fast dynamics.

At the same time, stock exchange trading has a function in the global economy. It provides companies with financial resources and negotiates the value of companies. As a society, however, we could agree that nothing should be traded faster than a person can make decisions. In this context, a so-called transaction tax has long been discussed. For example, German chancellors Angela Merkel and Olaf Scholz have advocated for it at a European level. The mechanism is that a very small proportion of the turnover has to be paid for each stock transaction. It would make extremely frequent trading less attractive and to me seems like a very elegant way of preventing something unwanted, even if you do not set a direct limit. In terms of folding, you could just as easily set a limit for trading frequency and say, for example, that trading is only allowed once per second because that is in the order of magnitude of the human decision-making speed.

In terms of folding, it is particularly important to state transparently that the reason for this tax is not an indirect one. It is not being introduced to finance a social task, but to prevent the danger of self-amplification and thus the risk of a system collapse.

8.7 The Folding Society

Let us leave aside the nanosecond trade again and consider what would happen if we introduced the two original folding limits I proposed earlier in the chapter. If, on the one hand, no one is allowed to earn more than a hundred times as much as another person, i.e. we limit the annual income to a very high number, say two million; and if we then allow at most this maximum annual income to be inherited by one person. So, each child is allowed to inherit up to two million, but no more. What would happen?

For almost everyone, nothing would change directly at all. Everyone I know would probably pursue their ambitions with the same intensity as before. Stock market traders would continue to try to get rich. Nurses would continue to help people. But it would probably no longer be worth charging the highest possible rents, because landlords would pay ever higher taxes on the income from these rents. The so-called marginal profit would become smaller and smaller with a higher income. As a result, businesses and people would have to pay lower rents. It would still be worth investing money and renovating houses. The incentive to do this would slowly decrease from a net annual income of one million and would be zero at two million. Prosperity would be spread across more shoulders, while the drive to earn this prosperity would be rekindled in each generation.

What is the folding in this idea? Well, first of all, it is simply that the money would be folded back into society at the end of a person's life. The introduction of an income limit, however high it may be, would radiate into all areas of society. Just as the realization that the Earth is not at the centre of the universe has changed the way we see ourselves. It matters whether you live in a society that makes it possible and desirable in principle to strive upwards to infinity, or in one that defines a balance of motion and relaxation as good. In practical terms, the taxation of each individual would make it financially worthwhile for both partners in a family to work, as this would double the income limit for the family – not because the family is allowed to have more income, but because both parents are allowed to have one income each.

Perhaps the working life would be extended and the working week reduced at the same time? The wealth limit would somewhat devalue the meaning of money in life, but it would not devaluate it completely, of course. Some would continue to pursue a maximum-income path, because it would still be possible to become very rich. But the outflow of wealth up into a layer of the super-rich would be stopped. This money would always be folded back into the middle of society and would have to be acquired again and again in each generation. The slight shift away from a wealth incentive would possibly increase the search for other meaningful goals, such as the search for knowledge, the creation of art or fulfilment via interaction with other people, for example in care.

This is looking into a crystal ball; it is difficult to predict exactly what would happen and how social developments would change. What is crucial is that a certain balance is maintained between all parts of society and its members. I am convinced that this balance is existential for the preservation of our prosperity and our democracy.

9 The Path to Accord

> Do not try and bend the spoon. That's impossible. Instead only try to realize the truth.
> What's the truth?
> There is no spoon.
> *Rowan Witt as the Spoon Boy with Keanu Reeves as Neo in "The Matrix" (1999)*

This book does not provide any practical solutions for a new societal agreement. The upheavals I describe here are too fundamental for that, the book is too short, and I am not qualified enough to do so. The practical solutions must emerge from a democratic process in which the expertise of some and the creativity of all are combined. The narrative of folding can help to give space to creativity and inspire it. The laws and rules must, of course, be thought over, discussed and developed by elected representatives of the people, supported by expert knowledge.

With this book, I am trying to provide a narrative that replaces the idea of growth, which has shaped our thinking for decades, if not centuries, but is now destroying our society and our planet through a number of undesirable developments and excesses. At its core, the idea of growth implies that the meaning of our lives is linked to the accumulation of more and more – so that the house we live in is bigger than our parents'. Material growth into bigger and more destroys our Earth and therefore our freedom. At the same time, the growth narrative has long proved its worth as a driver of our progress. Thus there are good reasons not to give it up lightly.

The new narrative can therefore not simply cancel out the old one by slowing us down. A philosophy of life that prompts us to get up in the morning and say "It's best if I don't do anything today" and "My day today is going to be the same as yesterday" will not work. Because rationality and reason alone is not enough to drive us. It is a control, not a drive.

The dilemma that needs to be resolved is that we need opportunities for development and progress that do not involve destruction. This solution actually requires a new idea. The idea of folding is not new in itself. It already exists in many areas of our lives. In art and culture, development has been based on the principle of folding for thousands of years, in physics and mathematics for centuries, and it has also been applied in the economy without being named as such. It cannot be ruled out that someone has already formulated this idea in a similar way. What is certain, however, is that the idea has not yet reached a broad social base.

It would be good, I am convinced, if we could agree on this new narrative. Folding is something that sensible communists can agree on with sensible capitalists together with sensible ecologically minded people, and even the pure pragmatists can be convinced. So if one of the following arguments convinces you that is enough, you do not have to agree with all of them.

9.1 Arguments for Capitalists

With regard to my proposal to limit the size of companies and the inequality of wealth, some people may have thought that this was communism. But a society in which you can earn two million euros net a year – i.e. one person can earn a hundred times more than another – and in which the state does not own means of production, is not a communist society. At least not one that corresponds to the original ideas of Marx or Engels or even Lenin or Luxemburg. Folding merely limits the excesses of capitalist developments, but it does not restrict the entrepreneurial freedom of 99 percent of the self-employed one bit. Nor does it eliminate every possibility of growth in terms of value creation. In fact, it only folds the anti-competitive extremes created by exponential growth back into society – extremes and excesses that were only achieved after the end of the Cold War and the associated systemic competition, when capitalism was transformed into unbridled turbo-capitalism. These excesses are now to be controlled by folding not in a non-transparent and sudden manner, but by setting transparent and clear rules. They are intended to limit inequality in society and the economy without eliminating it.

An understanding of scale is fundamentally important here. The growth of companies will not be curtailed as long as it does not conflict with democratic interests. What is new is the decision to seriously control undesirable developments that have now become apparent in many countries: namely the fact that the primacy of politics over the economy is being called into question by the power of some companies, and some extremely wealthy individuals, who are using their power to destroy the market and its competition as well as democracy.

The market economy depends on the existence of a functioning society. Only in a society can values be negotiated, needs develop, and values be protected. If we can agree that all of this should take place in a democratic form of government, then we must protect the market with its competition and the sovereignty of the people at the same time. Limiting the size of companies is only meant to serve these purposes. At the moment, companies are not limited since cartel offices are not a dynamical part of the economic system and thereby not effective. They are basically a socialist instrument in a capitalist operation. In order to maintain entrepreneurial decision-making power, companies must be taxed transparently in such a way that it is not worth exceeding certain limits. The specific value for this limit should not be based on a national budget, but on something like an international average (e.g. the G7 countries), so that companies from very wealthy economic nations do not automatically become the largest, while others remain globally uncompetitive.[1]

Anyone who believes in the power of the market can only welcome folding. After all, companies that are so big that they are *too big to fail*

---

[1] The limit here should be set globally so that multinational companies can be dealt with. However, this also shows that there can be no clear rule here that is based on the budget of just one country.

or even so big that they compete financially with the state in which they operate have already bid farewell to competition. No established medium-sized company or even a new start-up can compete with these mega-corporations. Competition has been eliminated.

Some people may argue that corporations such as Microsoft or Facebook were only founded a few decades ago and have established themselves on the market – that they too were once small start-up companies. That is true. But they did not have to compete against a mega-corporation in the same product area. They have opened up new market areas. The dynamic that arises when a mega-corporation is already on the market can be seen very clearly, for example, with Instagram. It began as a small start-up company and was bought by Facebook for one billion dollars shortly after it was founded. The competition was eliminated. As in the Socialist Unity Party of Eastern Germany[2] or the CSU in Bavaria,[3] this means that competition is only possible within the organization and is therefore susceptible to nepotism and corruption.

In fact, folding is simply the second half of the theory that has been missing from macroeconomics so far. In conventional growth models, the economy reaches equilibrium when technology is not advancing and population growth is stagnant. Technological growth is often an externally prescribed variable, i.e. an externality, and is thus generally not subject to self-amplification dynamics in the original neoclassical theory.[4] In reality, the capital that goes into the technological development of lucrative ideas and concepts is a self-amplification factor. And thus, a theory of technological progress must also include self-amplification if it is to explain phenomena such as the growth of Microsoft, Facebook, Apple and Amazon.

2 Sozialistische Einheitspartei (SED).

3 Christlich-Soziale Union (CSU).

4 There is now a wealth of literature that deals with describing technological progress within the world of economic thought. However, this is not yet part of classical theory. In any case, a successful theory of technological progress, if it is possible, will have to include self-amplification processes if it wants to explain the explosion of knowledge over the last century and thus also the exponential growth of Microsoft, Facebook and Amazon.

We are observing both an acceleration of technological progress and an expansion of the economic area across the entire globe. As a result, the equilibrium conditions of a conventional growth model are, if not undermined, then shifted to such an extent that this equilibrium is only reached after a quasi-exponential growth phase and only when practically the entire world has been penetrated.[5]

Anyone who believes in competition and freedom as fundamental social forces has an interest in ensuring that these forces are preserved. However, the self-amplification within the capitalist economic system abolishes precisely these, its own driving forces. We can preserve them by giving everyone a fresh and equal start at the beginning of their working life and by keeping the size of companies within a competitive range.

More than eighty years have passed since the Second World War. That is roughly three generations. If we assume for a moment that one generation is the time scale for our exponential growth, then we are now at a crossroads. Within the first generation, exponential growth still feels linear (Figure 3). Those who achieve more earn more. In the second generation, you can already see the advantage that those who were born rich have. They start with different prerequisites and an injustice begins to emerge. In the third generation, those who started out with slightly better starting conditions have built up their advantage to such an extent that their success becomes unattainable for the rest of society. Even if it is possible today to enter the society of the super-rich within a generation, this is reserved for those who benefit from self-amplification processes, such as top managers and soccer stars. There is nothing wrong with that. It just should not distract us from the fact that success within the third generation no longer depends on

[5] In the frequently used neoclassical theory with a so-called Cobb–Douglas production function, this results in sub-exponential growth, which is based on the assumption that the effect of capital on growth decreases with higher capital. Whether this is a sensible assumption for an economy can be debated. However, this is about the situation in which a company that actually obeys economic laws becomes so large that it begins to dominate the macroeconomy. The macroeconomic description is highly unlikely to be suitable for the phase of development from start-up to mega-corporation, and the question of how a theory has to be changed when it can no longer be assumed that an economy consists of a large number of companies, but of a few, is a very exciting one. Because this is where the law of large numbers, of statistics, breaks down and the world becomes complex.

performance. This should bother people who believe in the market. Folding can fix that.

9.2 Arguments for Communists

I can understand anyone who harbours a deep mistrust of capitalism and the market economy. In its unbridled form, this system is one that places competition, and therefore supposedly efficiency, above human dignity. There are countless regions in the world and in these countless social groups that are forced into undignified living conditions because of the market economy. The self-amplification growth of capital cements the differences in prosperity and widens them further. Unlimited capitalism abolishes its own virtues. Exponential growth destroys competition between companies. Exponential growth of private property has generated a class that operates outside the rest of society through unlimited income and inheritance. At the same time, the exponential growth in the consumption of raw materials has caused global climate change and an unimaginable extinction of species.

I understand very well that people have lost trust in the idea that this system can be reformed due to the situation we find ourselves in globally. I can understand the call for a fundamentally different system. But it can only be the first step to point out and name the grievances. Political and social movements often stop at this point, people settle into their critical bubble and wait for the next generation to solve it.

If we want to make progress, we have to ask what this other, this new system should look like. It is clear that it is not possible to keep capitalism humane[6] if the tax system allows not only companies to

---

[6] When looking at the income or wealth data of different countries and comparing them within or between countries, it is common to present them in graphs on a so-called logarithmic scale. On such a scale, 1,000 euros is just as far away from 100 euros as it is from 10,000 euros. However, this metric naturally does not correspond to human reality. It is only used because the differences between people and countries are so great that it is otherwise impossible to get a real overview of the data. As long as the differences are so great that we have to do this, something big is wrong. A very helpful database for this is the World Inequality Database portal co-run by French economist Thomas Piketty: https://wid.world.

have more money than some countries, but even individuals to be richer than the national budgets of some countries. But what is the solution?

Folding has the potential to provide this new system. It limits the wealth gap between people. At the same time, the economic system of folding is the opposite of a planned economy. I can understand why communist theorists believe that society should be supplied by state production planned according to the people's needs. However, I believe that we have now understood that this is an overestimation of the state's capabilities and is highly susceptible to corruption. Moreover, our world is so complex that institutions seem to be constantly lagging behind developments. The answer to the world's current problems should not be to slow down development, even if this may seem very attractive in the age of digitalization and globalization. Instead, development should be controlled in the way it was once intended: The state creates laws that set the rules in a democratic and transparent process. These rules must not come across as overly bureaucratic micromanagement.

The question is: What should a new social system achieve? It should create progress for people's prosperity, but keep the differences between people reasonable. I think it would be unfair to eliminate differences completely. However, to ensure that everyone is rewarded according to their own performance, we must limit inheritance and make the starting conditions more similar.

The question of ownership of means of production remains. If companies worth more than two million can no longer be inherited as a whole, then we are moving towards everyone sharing in the profits of economic development. If individuals can no longer accumulate large blocks of shares because income per year is limited and inheritance is also limited, this means a diversification of shareholders. In contrast to the concentration of wealth over time, as is happening today, we will see a redistribution of wealth among the population in each generation: a democratization of the economy through shared ownership in companies. This part of the stock market is not the problem at the moment. What is problematic and dangerous for democracy is the accumulation of shares by major shareholders and the associated income without benefits.

Accepting poverty for all in order to enforce equality cannot be the solution. We must allow development towards prosperity and maintain a clear incentive system for performance, but prevent excessive, undignified differences.

9.3 Arguments for Sustainability

We need progress, not only to fight poverty in the world, but also if we want to live sustainably on our planet. In the climate debate, the focus is on disasters that are coming our way. But we can turn the prevention of a dystopia into a utopia, with the positive narrative of the co-evolution of humans and nature. This concept is extensive, and I would like to highlight just two aspects here. If we manage to generate our energy supply entirely from renewable sources, we will be able to generate much more energy[7] than we do today, because the amount of solar energy[8] is basically infinite. This energy is available to us in the most usable form of all, namely as electricity. In this respect too, wind and solar energy are superior to thermal power plants. When generating electricity, they do not take the detour via heat generation and thus avoid the problem of finite efficiency.[9] However, if we have an unlimited supply of energy, then we really can finally start to tackle our enormous

7 Of course, energy is not created, but rather transferred from a state of higher entropy to a lower one. We can then do more with this "ordered" energy. In principle, it is not possible to lower the entropy of a system unless energy is supplied from outside the system. This means that ultimately the universe is heading towards a kind of heat death. But let us just focus on life on Earth. I think that is a wonderful task. The universe has to be saved by someone else.

8 This explicitly includes the wind energy generated by the different strength of solar influx at different latitudes. Winds and ocean currents are generated by the spatially varying distribution of solar radiation on Earth and are therefore also solar energy to a certain extent.

9 All power plants that generate electricity from heat require a heat difference that drives a turbine in some form. A maximum efficiency, the so-called Carnot efficiency $\epsilon_{Carnot} = \frac{T_{hot} - T_{cold}}{T_{hot}}$, can be derived from the laws of thermodynamics. Although this increases with the temperature difference that can be created, it is still low. This means that more than half of the energy contained in coal, for example, is lost as waste heat and creates local environmental problems. During heatwaves caused by climate change, for example, these power plants have a cooling problem and initially become more inefficient and eventually have to be shut down. This applies to coal, gas, oil and nuclear power plants.

recycling problem. The second law of thermodynamics implies that you can only really recycle materials if you put additional energy into it. If this energy is available, then we can produce in such a way that we only use materials that have already been used. The aim must be for every cell phone to be made exclusively from materials that have already been used. At the end of its service life, it will then be completely returned to the cycle. If we manage to stop extracting raw materials from nature, then we have the chance to achieve a stable balance with the planet we live on. Industrial circles have often dismissed ecological aspects as idealistic and therefore unrealistic, but there is no harsher reality than the fact that you cannot extract materials from a finite planet indefinitely.

The end of the fossil fuel era can be the beginning of a real recycling solution. As a global community, we are striving to ensure that no more oil, gas or coal is extracted from nature and burned. Once we have created the political and economic instruments to achieve this globally, and we are currently in the process of doing so, then this is the roadmap for cessation of extracting other materials from nature. Plastic bans in many European countries are the first step.

If we combine this idea with the projected population development of the Earth, then we may have a future. Population growth is a self-amplification process as long as the number of births is greater than the death rate. If you look at the birth rates in Europe and the US, there have been signs of a change for decades. It seems that wherever women in a society are free to make decisions about their own lives, a balance is achieved that we can live with. When women's direct and indirect dependence on men and social constraints are reduced, some women seem to choose to have children and others not. This includes freedom from religious and social constraints, but above all education and financial independence. These are values that we strive for far beyond the sustainability problem. It is thus likely that increasing prosperity will stabilize the world's population if it is accompanied with enlightenment and democracy. If we achieve this and have sufficient energy available, then there is good reason to hope that we will succeed in reducing the human footprint on Earth – so much so that we can live in harmony with the planet.

In the eighties and nineties of the last century, the environmental movement initially formed not because of climate change, but primarily as a reaction to the chemical destruction of the environment by humans. At that time, the environmental issues were acid dumping in the North Sea, the collapse of the Baltic Sea ecosystem, in which marine life was barely possible, and "acid rain," which was massively attacking the forests. The challenges were relatively small in comparison to global warming, but the counter arguments put forward by industry were similar to those used today.

Sensible policies in Western democracies have succeeded in greatly reducing these problems. We now have laws in both the USA and Europe against the dumping of waste into the environment. There are limits on exhaust fumes from domestic and industrial chimneys. These regulations are certainly not perfect, but they have taken us a big step forward and we are now looking at other aspects. We have introduced limits and the economy has not gone under. It has found a way to exist within these boundaries and create something new.

From a folding point of view, the main criticism of past regulations is that they were quite complicated and detailed. In terms of folding, simple rules are advantageous because they can be transparently incorporated into the dynamics of the system. For example, a law could be passed stating that no substances may be released into nature that harm the flora and the fauna, including humans. It may well be that such a law already exists in some countries. It is crucial to transfer the risk assessment to the polluter instead of burdening the state and its authorities with the search for pollutants.

In all these considerations, it is important for me to make it clear that I do not believe that humanity's footprint has to disappear completely. We naturally have a right to live on this planet and to take up space. But the way we are currently doing it is disastrous. Folding with two, perhaps even three ecological folding boundaries could point the way to transformation into a sustainable society.

9.4 Arguments for Pragmatists

The world has become much more complex since the time in which we developed our social and economic systems. While it may have seemed possible in the 19th and early 20th century for a state to plan a country's economy centrally, it has been shown that even then this concept did not work. Planning regularly fails to assess all the needs and necessities arising in a society in advance, and then collapses completely when it is implemented.

We have therefore in most countries decided for a market and against a planned economy and have delegated the easing of social injustices caused by the market to increasingly detailed legislation. The more detailed the laws, the less clear they become to the general public. This leads to a dolefulness within the population, who no longer understand the rules. Too much bureaucracy and micromanagement by the state are met with disapproval. In addition, the weaker members of society are generally at a disadvantage when the rules become complicated. We should remind ourselves every now and then that legislation is only meant to set the framework within which action can be taken. It need not and must not prescribe action in detail. A free society with clear rules that prohibit certain action is better at finding solutions than the state alone.

In this sense, the folding is a deregulation, although it begins with the setting of hard limits. However, if things are only prohibited on a large scale, i.e. at the extreme edges of self-amplification processes, and micromanagement is avoided, this induces a modern way of solution and problem finding. The population, the economy, science and culture are left to find their own paths into the future. In principle, this is already the case, but we need to understand that borders inspire this solution finding and do not prevent it, as long as they do not prescribe the path, i.e. become micromanagement.

Just as you can trust that a room will be ventilated when you open the window and that the fresh air will reach every corner of the room, you can also count on humanity finding solutions for the future if you let it. Erroneous paths are taken and discarded, but the functioning, viable paths remain. This is an ergodic solution finding process, induced by folding. The prohibitions must start with what society does not want for moral and ethical reasons. However, it is dangerous to ban things that we merely perceive to lead into the wrong direction. This prevents possible solutions simply because we cannot imagine that they could be successful in the short term. Here are a few examples: You do not ban flying, you ban carbon dioxide and other pollutant emissions. You do not ban electricity generation, you ban the production of nuclear waste. You do not ban packaging, you ban plastic. Even if this may only appear to be a semantic difference in some cases, this approach describes a fundamental difference to current policy, which in many cases also has direct consequences.

Entrepreneurs are familiar with solving problems and, above all, creating innovative, new solutions within a framework that allows freedom and provides incentives. It is the most powerful way into the future. The trick is to strike the right balance between freedom and limitation.

The folding limits are based on decisions that are based on certain fundamental values that we agree on as a society. A world without human rights is conceivable and possible, as the Chinese government is increasingly openly demonstrating. Nevertheless, the borders we set have a universal claim; if nothing else this can be seen from their unbroken appeal. Not only do people from all over the world migrate to countries with a democratic constitution, but there are also prisoners in numerous dictatorships who are standing up for human rights with their lives.

When I propose new folding limits here, it is important for me to emphasize with regard to the two ecological folding boundaries that I am taking a fundamentally different path than most representatives of the ecology movement. The debates about a sustainable way of life often revolve around our everyday actions. Many of those who reject the environmental movement are bothered by the feeling of being patronized. Some in the ecological movement would prefer to go so far as to prescribe people's value system: I should no longer be a car lover, but like cycling, and although I like schnitzel, I should prefer vegetables. It is precisely this ecological moralism that drives others to reject any form of ecologically sensible policy. Of course, I do not have the right to dictate to another person what they should like or dislike. Prescribing other people's feeling is just as sensible as prohibiting the climate from heating up. It does not work. However, I do have the right to demand that people do not destroy the common goods that we all share. Everything that nature provides for our survival, including its environmental conditions, is a common good. The consequence of this view is that we are not allowed to ban flying, but are allowed to ban emitting CO_2.

The folding limits therefore offer a way out of this paternalistic dilemma. They do not dictate in any way what my value system should look like, but simply say: You must not harm others. Or to be more specific: Whatever we do, we must do in the foreseeable future without emitting CO_2, and perhaps in the more distant future without using new resources. If we succeed in switching to 100 percent renewable energies, recycled materials and renewable raw materials, then it will be perfectly fine to travel or drive a Porsche. The same applies to the economic folding limits that I propose. They should not restrict the freedom to develop, become rich and enjoy life. On the contrary, I believe that limiting inequality is necessary in order to maintain our free way of life and our prosperity in the future.

9.5 What We Can Agree On

Almost eighty years after the United Nations Charter laid the foundations for a global community that agreed on certain globally applicable rights and values – one could say the first globally effective folding limits – our social discourses are now divided and hardened in many countries. Not only the global community itself, but also societies within states are dividing into political camps with seemingly irreconcilable differences. Radical anti-democratic movements are gaining strength again, and in many countries they have already been elected into government or are even leading it. There may be many reasons for this development. What is clear, however, is that certain self-amplification processes within our democratic system are slowly beginning to break down not only the ecological limits, but also the social contracts that we once agree to. We have to do something.

But we also *can* do something. After the Second World War, we agreed on a few basic rules as a community of states. Two approaches to practical implementation emerged. Even if the socialist or communist path was associated with a dictatorial form of government and the governments of these states trampled down most of these goals, the existence of this alternative was for a long time an incentive for the Western world to uphold its own social standards. In the 1970s, many Western countries had tax rates of up to 70 percent for very high incomes (in the USA, this tax rate even applied until 1982). It was only when the communist alternative disappeared that a turbo-capitalism was unleashed in the Western democracies, destroying the hope for global peace and prosperity that was cherished in 1990, within just a few decades. With the founding of the World Trade Organization in 1995, globalized trade took on a new dimension. The associated self-amplification processes in the globalized economy are unfolding their full force. Legislation, which is mostly limited to nation states, can no longer compete with their power.

Many see the problem in globalization and international trade relations, through which we as a society have become entangled in ever more opaque interdependencies and dependencies, and they call for a return to economic confinement within national borders. The excessive demands placed on society by globalization are one of the causes used to explain the worldwide rise of right-wing populism. On the other hand, free market advocates counter that global prosperity has increased with every decade since the foundation of the World Trade Organization. What is overlooked in this debate is that the major problems are not caused by the global economy itself, but by its unregulated self-amplification processes. Trade brings huge profits at every level for everyone involved. However, this is only true as long as the balance of power and wealth between the participants is indeed balanced. Unleashed, self-amplification growth in the economy and deregulated financial markets tip this balance.

It is time to rediscover balance and learn from the past. By folding, I am describing a way to prevent the destruction of our finite planet and at the same time the tearing apart of our society, without eliminating growth as a necessary incentive system. A development into a future society that slowly but steadily adapts its value system to new challenges, whether these challenges consist of the finite nature of our planet or new technological achievements. The acceptance of limits, for example our planetary boundaries but also limits in inequality, is a necessary and currently the most important addition to human rights and our democratic constitution and states of law.

I invite you to imagine a world in which we have agreed on five new folding limits in addition to the human rights enshrined in many national constitutions:

1. **End the burning of fossil fuels:** In order to comply with the Paris Climate Agreement, to which 195 countries have agreed, CO_2 emissions worldwide must be reduced to zero within the next twenty years.[10]
2. **End the extraction of raw materials:** Our planet is finite, and therefore at some point no more raw materials may be extracted from it.[11]
3. **Limiting the size of companies:** The sovereign of a country is its population. The primacy of politics over the economy applies,

[10] As described in Chapter 6, European emissions trading is an implementation of this limit designed to help the economy incorporate the transformation to carbon-free production competitively. It is now largely effective in the sectors in which it has been implemented. It must be strengthened, extended to all sectors and implemented consistently.

[11] This folding limit is a logical and physically clear conclusion from the obvious finiteness of our planet. Sooner or later it will be demanded by reality, whether we set it or not. Our production will then have to be based entirely on renewable and recycled products. The implementation of this limit will generate an enormous surge in innovation (Chapter 6).

and therefore no company may become larger and more powerful than the countries in which it operates.[12]

4. **Limitation of inheritance:** People should start life with as many equal opportunities as possible, which is why the inheritance that goes to a person must be limited. This is exclusively about preventing the inheritance of great wealth.[13]
5. **Limiting the income gap:** The basis of our well-being is the existence of a common society. To ensure equality before the law and in voting, the ratio of incomes should be limited. This is not about preventing wealth, but about preventing our society from being torn apart.[14]

Unlike many other larger and smaller boundaries that we set for our actions in the form of regulations and laws, these folding limits describe a vision: They direct all individual, corporate and political developments towards the goal of a sustainable future in which we can maintain and even increase the prosperity we have achieved over centuries or even millennia, not only ecologically, but also socially and economically. As happened in the past with the declaration of human rights, our value system will also adapt. We will redefine what we perceive as prosperity. It is crucial that this reorientation is not predetermined, but can unfold freely. Only developments that endanger our coexistence will be limited.

If we succeed in agreeing on such new folding limits, it will also be necessary to learn from experience. The principle of folding only works if a development is really stopped by the set limit. If the ping-pong ball from the prologue can puncture the wall against which it is flying,

[12] As described in Chapter 7, this limit would only apply to mega-corporations, as it is not a matter of restricting the growth of companies in principle, but of protecting government sovereignty and preventing the destruction of competition through the formation of monopolies. The effective company cap could be in the order of 50 billion euros in turnover.

[13] As described in Chapter 8, the scale is decisive here. The maximum inheritance could be based on the maximum annual income, for example EUR 2,000,000 in a country like Germany, the UK or the US.

[14] Here too, as described in Chapter 8, the scale is decisive. The ratio of maximum income to minimum income could be limited to 100. With a minimum annual income of EUR 20,000, this would mean a maximum annual net-income of EUR 2,000,000.

it will not change direction, it will not fold its trajectory back into space. This means that folding limits must be hard, absolutely irrevocable boundaries. We have already experienced this with human rights, which have been repeatedly circumvented since their introduction. The national and European supply chain laws are attempts to prevent such circumvention. With regard to emissions trading, the EU is also currently developing a political instrument, the so-called Carbon Border Adjustment, which is basically a supply chain law for carbon emissions and is intended to prevent companies from simply emitting CO_2 outside the EU or purchasing products with a high carbon footprint from outside.

We urgently need these kinds of supply chain laws. I would like to propose a generally valid formulation of this folding limit of folding limits, a kind of generalized supply chain law, as follows:

The laws of a constitutional state also apply to imported products, and therefore only products that comply with the fundamental laws of a legislative unit may be sold within the jurisdiction of this legislative unit, be it a country or the European Union.

Of course, the folding limits I have suggested are not the only ones that can be imagined, and certainly the goals described in a vision cannot be achieved overnight. But if we manage to further develop this vision and then implement it (which we can), "What a wonderful world this could be."

Great Thanks

go to

Hans Joachim Schellnhuber, who has long seen the solution to our problems in the application of the theory of non-linear dynamics. I am indebted to you, John, because you gave me the freedom to do research so early in my career and created an institute that supports, promotes and endures this spirit of free research.

Stefan Rahmstorf, who has been fighting for the climate with incredible integrity and strength for decades, researching and defending the truth with scientific aplomb and brilliance. Thank you, too, for believing in me so early on and for putting up with our differences of opinion so sportingly for more than twenty years.

Ottmar Edenhofer, who gave me a fascination for economics and showed me how to think forcefully and intelligently about society.

Itamar Procaccia, who taught me that research is a creative process. Your classification of theoretical physicists as creators of culture was a revelation to me as a young scientist that has stayed with me to this day.

Jonas Viering, who taught me how to write and gave me so much more than this book.

Gunnar Luderer, Benjamin Bodirsky and Leonie Wenz, who I can turn to with the really difficult economic questions.

Literature

Bagwell, L. S., Bernheim, B. D., 1996. Veblen effects in a theory of conspicuous consumption. *Am. Econ. Rev.* 349–373.

Bak, P. 1999. *How Nature Works: The Science of Self-Organized Criticality*. Springer.

Bamber, J. L., Riva, R. E. M. M., Vermeersen, B. L. A., LeBrocq, A. M., 2009. Reassessment of the potential sea-level rise from a collapse of the west antarctic ice sheet. *Science* 324, 901–903.

Clapeyron, E. 1834. Mémoire sur la puissance motrice de la chaleur. *Journal de l'École Polytechnique* XXIIIe Cahier, Tome XIV.

Clausius, R. 1850. Über die bewegende Kraft der Wärme und die Gesetze, welche sich daraus für die Wärmelehre selbst ableiten lassen. *Annalen der Physik* 155 (4), S. 500–524.

Favier, L., *et al.*, 2014. Retreat of Pine Island Glacier controlled by marine ice-sheet instability. *Nat. Clim. Chang.* 5, 117–121.

Feldmann, J., Levermann, A., 2015. Collapse of the West Antarctic Ice Sheet after local destabilization of the Amundsen Basin. *Proc. Natl. Acad. Sci.* 112, 14191–14196.

Garbe, J., Albrecht, T., Levermann, A., Donges, J. F., Winkelmann, R., 2020. The hysteresis of the Antarctic Ice Sheet. *Nature* 585, 538–544.

Harari, Y. N., 2011. *Sapiens - A Brief History of Time.* Penguin Random House, UK.

IPCC-ExRes: Field, C. B., Barros, V., Stocker, T. F., Qin, D., Dokken, D. J., Ebi, K. L., Mastrandrea, M. D., Mach, K. J., Plattner, G.-K., Allen, S. K., Tignor, M., Midgley, P. M., 2012. *Managing the Risks of Extreme Events and Disasters to Advance Climate Change Adaptation – SREX Summary for Policymakers, A Special Report of Working Groups I and II of the Intergovernmental Panel on Climate Change.*

IPCC-WG1: Masson-Delmotte, V., Zhai, P., Pirani, A., Connors, S. L., Péan, C., Berger, S., Caud, N., Chen, Y., Goldfarb, L., Gomis, M. I.,

Huang, M., Leitzell, K., Lonnoy, E., Matthews, J. B. R., Maycock, T. K., Waterfield, T., Yelekçi, O., Yu, R., Zhou, B. (Eds.), 2021. *IPCC, 2021: Climate Change 2021: The Physical Science Basis. Contribution of Working Group I to the Sixth Assessment Report of the Intergovernmental Panel on Climate Change.* Cambridge University Press.

IPCC-WG2: Pörtner, H.-O., Roberts, D. C., Tignor, M., Poloczanska, E. S., Mintenbeck, K., Alegría, A., Craig, M., Langsdorf, S., Löschke, S., Möller, V., Okem, A., Rama, B. (Eds.), 2022. *IPCC, 2022: Climate Change 2022: Impacts, Adaptation, and Vulnerability. Contribution of Working Group II to the Sixth Assessment Report of the Intergovernmental Panel on Climate Change.* Cambridge University Press.

IPCC-WG3: Shukla, P. R., Skea, J., Slade, R., Khourdajie, A. Al, van Diemen, R., McCollum, D., Pathak, M., Some, S., Vyas, P., Fradera, R., Belkacemi, M., Hasija, A., Lisboa, G., Luz, S., Malley, J. (Eds.), 2022. *IPCC, 2022: Climate Change 2022: Mitigation of Climate Change. Contribution of Working Group III to the Sixth Assessment Report of the Intergovernmental Panel on Climate Change.* Cambridge University Press, Cambridge, UK and New York, USA.

Jensen, R. T., Miller, N. H., 2008. Giffen behavior and subsistence consumption. *Am. Econ. Rev.* 98, 1553–1577.

Joughin, I., Smith, B. E., Medley, B., 2014. Marine ice sheet collapse potentially under way for the thwaites glacier basin, West Antarctica. *Science* 344, 735–738.

Kornhuber, K., Coumou, D., Vogel, E., Lesk, C., Donges, J. F., Lehmann, J., Horton, R. M., 2020. Amplified Rossby waves enhance risk of concurrent heatwaves in major breadbasket regions. *Nat. Clim. Chang.* 10, 48–53.

Kornhuber, K., Osprey, S., Coumou, D., Petri, S., Petoukhov, V., Rahmstorf, S., Gray, L., 2019. Extreme weather events in early summer 2018 connected by a recurrent hemispheric wave-7 pattern. *Environ. Res. Lett.* 14.

Lenton, T. M., Held, H., Kriegler, E., Hall, J. W., Lucht, W., Rahmstorf, S., & Schellnhuber, H. J., 2008. Tipping elements in the Earth's climate system. *Proc. Natl. Acad. Sci. U.S.A.* 105(6) 1786–1793, https://doi.org/10.1073/pnas.0705414105.

Levermann, A., *et al.*, 2012. Potential climatic transitions with profound impact on Europe. *Clim. Change* 110, 845–878.

Levermann, A., Winkelmann, R., 2016. A simple equation for the surface-elevation feedback of ice sheets. *Cryosph.* 10, 1799–1807.

McKay, D. I. A., *et al.*, 2022. Exceeding 1.5 °C global warming could trigger multiple climate tipping points. *Science* 377, eabn7950.

Mercer, J. H., 1978. West Antarctic ice sheet and CO_2 greenhouse effect: a threat of disaster. *Nature* 271, 321.

Petoukhov, V., Rahmstorf, S., Petri, S., Schellnhuber, H. J., 2013. Quasiresonant amplification of planetary waves and recent Northern Hemisphere weather extremes. *Proc. Natl. Acad. Sci.* 110, 5336–5341.

Rahmstorf, S., 1996. On the freshwater forcing and transport of the Atlantic thermohaline circulation. *Clim. Dyn.* 12, 799–811.

Raymond, C., Matthews, T., Horton, R. M., 2020. The emergence of heat and humidity too severe for human tolerance. *Sci. Adv.* 6.

Riedel, N., Simmler, M., 2021. Large and influential: Firm size and governments' corporate tax rate choice. *Can. J. Econ.* 54, 812–839.

Rignot, E., Mouginot, J., Morlighem, M., Seroussi, H., Scheuchl, B., 2014. Widespread, rapid grounding line retreat of Pine Island, Thwaites, Smith, and Kohler glaciers, West Antarctica, from 1992 to 2011. *Geophys. Res. Lett.* 41, 3502–3509.

Robinson, A., Calov, R., Ganopolski, A., 2012. Multistability and critical thresholds of the Greenland ice sheet. *Nat. Clim. Chang.* 2, 429–432.

Rockström, J. *et al.*, 2009. Planetary boundaries: Exploring the safe operating space for humanity. *Ecol. Soc.* 14.

Schellnhuber, J. H., 2015. *Selbstverbrennung: Die fatale Dreiecksbeziehung zwischen Klima, Mensch und Kohlenstoff.* C. Bertelsmann Verlag.

Sherwood, S. C., Huber, M., 2010. An adaptability limit to climate change due to heat stress. *Proc. Natl. Acad. Sci. U. S. A.* 107, 9552–9555.

Veblen, T., 1899. *The theory of the leisure class: an economic study in the evolution of institutions.* Macmillan, New York, USA.

Weertman, J., 1974. Stability of the junction of an ice sheet and an ice shelf. *J. Glaciol.* 13, 3–11.

Wentland, K., 2023. The Effect of Industrial Diversification on Firm Taxes. *Account. Rev.* 98, 453–478.

Winkelmann, R., Levermann, A., Ridgwell, A., Caldeira, K., 2015. Combustion of available fossil fuel resources sufficient to eliminate the Antarctic Ice Sheet. *Sci. Adv.* 1, e1500589–e1500589.

Zimmerman, J. L., 1983. Taxes and Firm Size. *J. Account. & Econ.* 5, 119–149.

Index

www.ingramcontent.com/pod-product-compliance
Ingram Content Group UK Ltd.
Pitfield, Milton Keynes, MK11 3LW, UK
UKHW061550130926
8556IPUK00049B/890

9 781800 618985